GET THE POINT ACROSS

GET THE POINT ACROSS

200 Effective & Entertaining Stories for Speakers, Preachers and Teachers

Edited by
GRAHAM H TWELFTREE

SCB Publishers
MONARCH
Crowborough

Compilation copyright © Graham H Twelftree 1996

First published 1996

All rights reserved.
No part of this publication may be reproduced or
transmitted in any form or by any means, electronic
or mechanical, including photocopy, recording or any
information storage and retrieval system, without
permission in writing from the publisher.

British Library Cataloguing Data
A catalogue record for this book is available
from the British Library.

ISBN 1 85424 344 6

Co-published in South Africa with
SCB Publishers
Cornelis Struik House, 80 McKenzie Street
Cape Town 8001, South Africa.
Reg no 04/02203/06

Designed and produced by Bookprint Creative Services
P.O. Box 827, BN21 3YJ, England for
MONARCH PUBLICATIONS
Broadway House, The Broadway
Crowborough, East Sussex, TN6 1HQ
Printed in Great Britain.

To
Brian and Thora Anderson
and the People of
the Vineyard Christian Fellowship North Phoenix

CONTENTS

Preface	9
The Stories	11
Acknowledgements	225
Indexes	
Biblical Passages	233
Names, Places and Themes	245

PREFACE

The challenge for many speakers is to communciate effectively with young people: the Twenty-Somethings, Busters, or Generation Xers. Today we are talking to people whose minds are frequently informed by television, videos, computer games and the Internet. No longer are people learning primarily through seeing or hearing words and ideas. The clear, brief, high-impact image is the diet of modern minds.

We also share an era when objective truth and certainty are assumed to have been lost. No longer can anything be believed – except 'my' story.

Further, in modern times, there has never been a generation, such as this one, with an absence of meaningful relationships or so many broken relationships. Hope for new and meaningful relationships – with God and with each other in his family – can be conveyed through poignant stories.

The story is, then, increasingly important if we are going to communicate our message.

However, using (not reading out!) the stories that follow will need to involve personalizing, applying and retelling them with conviction – or passion, to use a contemporary catchword.

Graham Humphris (Adelaide), Phil Muston (Perth) and Steve Silvester (Nottingham) have read through these stories. As regular preachers, they were quick to point out the poor stories, but I must take responsibility for what follows, for I have sometimes not taken their advice!

In assembling these 200 stories I am grateful to all those who have sent, handed or told me stories. In my research, I have appreciated the help of Pastor Trevor Zweck and his staff at Luther Seminary (Adelaide) who have provided generous help and patiently answered a multitude of questions for me.

Unfortunately, the origins of many stories have been lost. However, as the acknowledgements at the end of the book show, I am grateful to those who could be traced and have allowed their story to be told here.

To make this book as 'user friendly' as possible, an important part is the themes and scriptures appended to each story. These, as well as the headings of each story, and many other key words and ideas are collected in the extensive indexes, helping readers to find stories quickly.

Tony and Jane Collins and their unseen team at Monarch have efficiently taken this book from my desk to yours. Thank you.

This book is dedicated to Brian and Thora Anderson and the people of the Vineyard Christian Fellowship North Phoenix. From 10 - 15 August 1994, their visit to our church changed our story for ever. Some details of that story are told in Wallace Boulton's book, *The Impact of Toronto* (Monarch, 1995).

On the way home in the car from worship each Sunday, Barbara, my wife, will invariably say something like, 'Well, that was a six'. Sometimes she will score my talk as high as a seven or an eight-and-a-half! Not surprisingly, my success will often have depended not only on biblical and theological fidelity but on the effective use of stories. I continue to treasure her companionship and correction.

Graham H Twelftree
Adelaide, 17 February 1996

The Stories

1: Abuse

When the author Dr John White was in junior high, a young married Christian youth worker invited him to stay for a week in his home in the country. The first night he was there he and the youth worker had devotions in their pyjamas on their knees beside the double bed he and his wife normally occupied. His friend's wife, for a reason that never occurred to John to question, was to sleep in a single room. John says: 'What followed made me feel embarrassed, fearful to offend, helpless, angry and sexually aroused, all at the same time. I was too embarrassed to go on resisting his attempts to seduce.'

John could not tell his parents for he did not have the language to describe what was happening to him and, after all, this man was a Christian leader.

John says that his encounter with the youth leader went on over a couple of years before he was able to break it off. Breaking it off was an important step for John and he says that his current sexual life is about as normal as it could be.

Themes: Homosexuality, Immorality, Inner healing, Sex, Sexual abuse, Youth ministry.

Scriptures: Leviticus 18:22; 20:13; Romans 1:24–27; 1 Corinthians 6:9–18; Galatians 5:16–24; Ephesians 5:3; 1 Thessalonians 4:3, 1 Timothy 1:8–11.

2: *Adultery*

Two travellers had to walk to a nearby country mansion when their car broke down. They knocked on the door, and a beautiful widow opened it. She said they were welcome to spend the night while her staff worked on the car. Months later, one of the travellers received a package containing legal documents. After surveying the contents, he immediately phoned the other traveller.

'When we were in the country, did you slip away in the night and go to that widow's bedroom?'

'Yes,' said the second traveller.

'Did you use my name?'

'Yes, but how did you find out?'

'Well, she has died and left me her entire estate.'

Themes: Death, Ethics, Humour, Inheritance, Sexuality, Travelling, Wills.

Scriptures: Exodus 20:14, Leviticus 20:10; Deuteronomy 5:18; Proverbs 6:32; Jeremiah 3:8; 5:7; 13:27; Hosea 2:1–5; Matthew 5:7–8; 19:9 Mark 7:21; 10:11, 19; John 8:1–11; 2 Peter 2:14.

3: Adultery

Around a country school in South Australia there were about twenty acres of trees. Through it went a winding dirt track, locally known as 'Lovers' Lane'. Saturday nights, young people would sneak through the dark and shine torches in the windows of the parked cars and there was great revelry on the part of the pranksters as young lovers were disturbed. One day, as some lads shone the torch in a car to give the lovers a fright; they got more than they bargained for. It was one of the lads who got a fright. In the car was his mother, caught in the very act of adultery with another man.

Themes: Ethics, Parenting, Sexuality.

Scriptures: Exodus 20:14; Leviticus 20:10; Deuteronomy 5:18; Proverbs 6:32; Jeremiah 3:8; 5:7; 13:27; Hosea 2:1–5; Matthew 5:7–8; Matthew 19:9; Mark 7:21; 10:11, 19; John 8:1–11; 2 Peter 2:14.

4: AIDS

Earvin 'Magic' Johnson is well over six feet tall. He is the all-American hero, worshipped like a god. He is a champion basketball player who has lived on a pedestal for years. But, on 7 November 1991, he announced his retirement from professional basketball. He had not long been married to his high school sweetheart Cookie. Cookie was already pregnant. Cookie said that they had sort of been together for fourteen years.

A few weeks after they married Magic had a blood test. It showed he was infected with HIV, the virus that can cause AIDS. When Magic told his pregnant wife, she was stunned and started to cry. They had married just a few weeks earlier. The next moment she slapped him with her hand. He explained that he had slept with women too numerous to know who had infected him. In fact, after he had arrived in LA in 1979, he had done his best to accommodate as many women as he could – most of them through unprotected sex.

'I told her that I'd understand if she wanted to leave me but she hushed my lips with a kiss,' he said.

Cookie said, 'We have been together on and off for the past fourteen years. Our love is so strong that I would never leave him to be alone with his pain. Not for one second did I consider packing my things.'

There was one sad comment made by Cookie, 'Everything's the same, except we can't have unprotected sex'.

Themes: Adultery, Fame, Heroes, Idols, Love, Marriage, Sex, Sexual ethics, Sport, Worship.

Scriptures: Exodus 20:14; Leviticus 20:10; Deuteronomy 5:18; Proverbs 6:32; Jeremiah 3:8; 5:7; 13:27; Hosea 2:1–5; Matthew 5:7–8; 19:9; Mark 7:21; 10:11, 19; Luke 13:1–5; John 8:1–11; Romans 1:18–32; 13:9; 2 Peter 2:14.

5: AIDS

A homosexual was dying of AIDS. Without disclosing his illness, he invited a minister to lunch. Halfway through their meal, the homosexual paused. He looked the minister in the eye, and blurted out,

'I am dying of AIDS'. Then, with tears in his eyes, the minister reached across the table and touched the homosexual's arm, 'I am sorry, I am truly sorry', he said. Later, the homosexual submitted his life to Jesus. He said this to the minister,

'Do you want to know why I have decided to receive Jesus? When I told you I was dying of AIDS, I was watching your body language. I wondered if you would quickly lean back, away from my face. Or if you would surreptitiously move your glass and your plate towards you . . . Instead of rejecting me, you reached out and touched me. Your eyes filled with tears . . . You accepted me. Then and there I decided that your God is the God I want to meet when I die.'

Themes: Acceptance, Compassion, Evangelism, God – meeting, Good Samaritan, Homosexuality, Kindness, Life – after death, Love – God's.

Scripture: Leviticus 19:18; Mark 12:31; Luke 10:25–37; 13:1 5; Romans 1:18–32; 12:20–21; 13:9; Galatians 6:2; James 2:8.

6: AIDS

An AIDS victim died. Sadly, no minister was interested in taking the funeral. Eventually the undertaker found a minister who was willing to conduct the ceremony. When the minister got to the funeral parlour he found about twenty five to thirty homosexual men waiting for him. They were in the room with the casket, just sitting as though they were frozen in their chairs. Each one of them faced straight ahead with glassy, unfocused eyes. Their hands were folded on their laps as though some teacher had ordered them to sit that way. In all the various parts of the funeral, at the parlour and at the graveside, not a word was spoken by any of those men. As the minister left the graveside he realised that the men were still standing frozen in their places. He went back to one of them and said, 'Is there anything I can do for you?' The man asked the minister to read the Twenty Third Psalm because he was hoping someone would read it at the funeral. So the Twenty Third Psalm was read. When he had finished a second man spoke, and asked for another passage of Scripture. He wanted to hear the passage about nothing separating us from the love of God. For almost an hour the minister stood by the graveside reading passages of Scripture for those homosexual men.

Themes: Acceptance, Bible – value of, Clergy, Compassion, Death, Evangelism, Funerals, Homosexuality, Kindness, Love, Parable – Good Samaritan.

Scriptures: Psalm 23; Luke 13:1–5; Romans 1:18–32; 8:31–39; 13:9; 2 Corinthians 1:3–7.

7: Appearances

A few years ago, Adele Gaboury was reported missing. Concerned neighbours informed the police. But a brother told police she had gone into a nursing home. Satisfied with that information, Gaboury's neighbours began watching her property. Michael Crowley noticed her mail. It was delivered through a slot in the door and it was piling high. When he opened the door, hundreds of pieces of mail drifted out. He notified the police, and the deliveries were stopped.

Adele's next-door neighbour was Eileen Dugan. She started paying her grandson $10 a fortnight to mow Adele's lawn. Later, Eileen Dugan's son noticed Adele's pipes had frozen. Water spilled out the door. The water authority was called to turn off the water. What no one had guessed was that all the while they'd been trying to help, Adele Gaboury had been inside her home.

The police investigated the house as health hazard. They were shocked to find her body. The press reported that the police believed Adele had died of natural causes four years previously.

Themes: Care, Death, Neglect, Neighbours, Servant evangelism.

Scriptures: Leviticus 19:18; Mark 12:31; Luke 10:25-37; Romans 13:9; Galatians 6:2.

8: Atonement

The story is told that Billy Graham, the great American evangelist, was once caught for speeding and received a ticket from the traffic cop. He went to the Sheriff's office to pay the fine. The Sheriff behind the desk took the piece of paper and did not react as he read the name William Franklin Graham. Then he looked up. He recognised Billy for he also was a Christian. They began to converse about Christian things.

Eventually the Sheriff got down to business. He opened his book and asked, 'How do you plead?'

'Guilty,' said Billy.

The Sheriff recorded the verdict in his register. 'That will be $150,' he said. Then the Sheriff got out his wallet, took out $150, wrote paid in full in the final column, left the money in the book and shut it.

Themes: Cross, Freedom, Jesus – his work, Ransom, Reconciliation, Redeemed.

Scriptures: Exodus 6:6; Psalm 77:14–15; Mark 10:45; Luke 24:21; John 1:29; 8:31–36; 1 Corinthians 1:30; 5:7; 6:19–20; 7:22–23; Galatians 3:13; 4:4–5; 5:1; Ephesians 1:7; 5:2; Titus 2:14; Hebrews 9:15; 1 Peter 1:18–19; 1 John 2:2.

9: Belonging

At one point in the story of *The Velveteen Rabbit* the toy horse gives a roundabout description of love to the toy rabbit. It goes like this.

'What is Real?' asked the rabbit one day... 'does it mean having things buzz inside of you and a stick-out handle?'

'Real isn't how you are made,' said the Skin Horse. 'It's a thing that happens to you. When a child loves you for a long, long time, not just to play with, but *really* loves you, then you become Real.'

'Does it hurt?' asked the Rabbit.

'Sometimes,' said the Skin Horse, for he was always truthful. 'When you are Real you don't mind being hurt.'

'Does it happen all at once, like being wound up,' the Rabbit asked, 'or bit by bit?'

'It doesn't happen all at once,' said the Skin Horse. 'You become. It takes a long time. That's why it doesn't often happen to people who break easily, or have sharp edges, or have to be carefully kept. Generally, by the time you are Real, most of your hair has been loved off, and your eyes drop out and you get loose in the joints and very shabby. But these things don't matter at all, because once you are Real you can't be ugly, except to people who don't understand.'

Themes: Acceptance, Family, Love, Marriage, Reality, Relationships, Rejection.

Scriptures: Leviticus 19:18; Mark 12:31; John 13:34; 15:12, 17; Romans 13:9–10; 1 Corinthians 13; Galatians 5:22; Ephesians 4:2; Colossians 3:12–14; Hebrews 13:1; 1 Peter 1:22; 1 John 2:7–11; 3:11–24; 4:7–21.

10: The Bible

A wealthy young man fell in love with BMW cars. As an expression of his devotion he bought a manual for one of the current models. He so much enjoyed reading it through that he decided to get up early each morning to read it more carefully, section by section. There were some sections that seemed particularly interesting; those he underlined, sometimes with different coloured pens. What seemed to be the more important sentences he began to memorise. In turn, there were a few lines he wrote out on small cards. He laminated them and put them on his mirror so he could see them when he shaved in the morning.

There were other people in his area who also had BMW handbooks. Our young man joined a group of these folk who met once a week in each others' homes to study their manuals. They would each bring different editions of the manual to compare what they said about various aspects of the BMW car.

In time, our young man decided it was time to go the next step. He enrolled in a night course to study German. He wanted to be able to read the manual in the original language. Yet, he had never bought a BMW car.

Themes: Bible – inspiration, Bible – memorising, Bible reading, Bible study, Personal devotions, God-knowing.

Scriptures: Psalm 14:1; Matthew 5:18; John 10:35; 2 Timothy 3:16–17; 2 Peter 1:20–21.

11: The Bible – life changing

In January 1994, 24-year-old Leon Booth of Runaway Bay, Queensland, Australia, threw himself in front of a fast-moving car. 'I couldn't see any point in living,' Leon said. The suicide bid resulted in several broken bones, a series of skin grafts and period of deep pain for his family who had already suffered through Leon's times in prison.

'I was tired of having no money and being unemployed. I drank away my problems, and then took every drug I could lay my hands on – pot, hash, marijuana, anything I could get,' says Leon.

During one prison term, he saw a psychiatrist for the first time. 'We knocked on every door looking for help, and Leon's suicide bid was a further desperate cry for help,' said Pam, his mother.

On his release from hospital Leon again visited a psychiatrist. But this one contacted the Rev John Tully, founder of New Life Ministry at Street Level Inc on Queensland's Gold Coast. John visited the family and introduced them to the Serenity New Testament with its integrated Twelve Steps to Recovery.

A week later he received a phone call from Leon's psychiatrist. 'I'm very impressed,' were the simple words used by the psychiatrist to describe what had been a dramatic turn-around in Leon's life.

'I always believed in God, though I didn't want anything to do with Bible-bashers', said Leon, adding quickly, 'but what I am reading in the New Testament applies to so much of my own life that my whole outlook has changed.' And Leon's mother says, 'Leon no longer hates us as he did before.'

Themes: Bible – importance of, Conversion, Family life, Suicide, Twelve Steps to Recovery.

Scriptures: 1 Kings 22–23; Psalm 14:1; Matthew 5:18; John 10:35; 2 Timothy 3:16–17; 2 Peter 1:20–21.

12: Bible – life changing

Ted McDonough lives in Moree in New South Wales. One day Ted was dumping some of his rubbish at the local 'tip' when he noticed a small New Testament in very good condition. Ted was not a religious man, but he picked it up saying to himself, 'You're too good to be left on a scrap heap'. And he put the book in his pocket.

Years later, when Ted's personal life and marriage problems caused him to question the meaning of life he decided to go to church. So, one Sunday morning he got up early, got dressed very carefully and went off to the local church. Ted then lived in a small town and the Christians did not have church every week and the church was shut. He went home and hunted for and found the New Testament he had picked up in the dump years before. In its pages Ted found forgiveness and a new life.

Themes: Bible – influence of , Bible – value of, Conversion, Forgiveness, Life – meaning of, New life.

Scriptures: 1 Kings 22–23; Psalm 14:1; Matthew 5:18; John 10:35; 2 Timothy 3:16–17; 2 Peter 1:20–21.

13: Birth

Elizabeth Berg kept a journal when she became a parent. She wrote of her experience.

> I still can't believe you're here. When I wake up in the morning, I automatically put my hand to my stomach, looking for the shape that was there when you were inside me. Then I remember that you are born, here, alive on your own, and I feel thrilled. I worry about you, lost-looking in a crib that seems gigantic. I check on you a million times a day as you sleep there . . . I am glad to have you out in the world with me at last . . . You wake up to nurse at night, and I rush down the dark hall to see you, happy for the excuse to hold you again . . . Sometimes when I come back to bed, your father is awake and asks me how you are. And I say you are fine, you are perfect. He holds me then, presses me against him. There is the humiliating rustle of my paper products: breast shields, the enormous sanitary pads I wear. I am not exactly sexy any more. But he seems not to mind. We are doing other things now, when we hold each other. We are celebrating the fact of you, lying asleep in the next room.

Themes: Babies, Birth, Christmas, God – his love, God – as parent, Mothers, Parenting.

Scriptures: Psalm 113:5–9; Matthew 23:37; Mark 14:36, Luke 15:11–32; John 1:12; 3:16; 15:19; 16:27; 17:23; Romans 8:15; 1 Corinthians 13:4–7; Galatians 2:20; 4:6; Ephesians 5:2, 25; 2 Thessalonians 2:16–17; I John 4:7 19.

14: Broken

The royal palace in Tehran, Iran, is breathtakingly beautiful. A visitor stepping into the palace is surrounded with millions of pieces of glittering sparkling glass. It appears as if the domed ceiling, the side walls and columns are diamond covered and not cut glass; however, they are all small pieces of mirrors. The edges of the myriad of little mirrors reflect prism light, throwing out the colours of the rainbow. Spectacular!

Here is how it happened. When the royal palace was planned the architects ordered mirrors to cover the entrance walls. When the mirrors arrived, it was found that they had all been broken in transit. There were thousands of pieces of smashed mirrors. They were going to dispose of them all when one creative man said, 'No, maybe it will be more beautiful because they are broken.'

He took some of the larger pieces and smashed them also and fitted them together like an abstract mosaic. Today, the palace is beautiful beyond words, awash with sparkling rainbow colours.

Themes: Beauty, Creation, Creativity, God's creativity, Inner healing, Opportunities, Past hurts, Recreation.

Scriptures: Genesis 1:1–2; Job 38:4–7; Psalms 19:1–4; 33:6, 9; 90:2; 102:25 Isaiah 40:22, 26, 28; 42:5; 45:18; Jeremiah 10:12–16; Amos 4:13; Acts 17:24; Romans 1:20; 12:2; 2 Corinthians 4:16; 5:17; Galatians 6:15; Ephesians 2:1–10; Titus 3:5.

15: Call

Every June, when the National Basketball Association holds its annual draft of college players, hundreds of players, good enough to be eligible for the draft, sit by their telephones anxiously awaiting a call that will inform them that they've been picked by one of the pro teams. Very few athletes receive a call. An article on the sports page of the Seattle *Post-Intelligencer* (29 June, 1986) states that only one in 12,000 basketball players gets a call that will land them on the starting five of a pro basketball team. That means that for every athlete chosen, 11,999 basketball players do not receive a call.

> **Themes:** Assurance, Discipleship, Election, Evangelism, God – his call, Life – purpose, Mission, Prayer – answers, Predestination.
>
> **Scriptures:** Isaiah 6:1–13; Jeremiah 1:4–19; Matthew 10:1–15; 28:16–20; Mark 3:13–15; 6:6–13; Luke 6:12–13; 9:1–6; 10:1–20; 24:45–49; Acts 1:8.

16: Cancer

A TV producer wanted to produce a very special programme. He obtained permission from a cancer specialist to place cameras in his clinic. He also gained approval from three patients – two men and a woman. He captured on film the moment each of them learned they were afflicted with a malignant cancer in its later stages. Their initial shock, disbelief, fear and anger are all there, graphically recorded in detail.

Then the documentary team followed these three families through the treatment process. The film records the ups and downs, the hopes and disappointments, the pain and the terror. What is interesting is the different ways the three people faced their suffering. Two of them reacted with anger and bitterness. They not only fought their disease, they seemed to be war with everyone else. Their personal relationships, and even their marriages, were shaken – especially as the end drew near.

But the third person was different. He was a humble black man from the inner city. His love for the Lord was so profound it was reflected in everything he said. When he and his wife were told he had only a few months to live, they revealed no panic. They quietly asked the doctor what it all meant. When he had explained the treatment programme and what they could anticipate, they politely thanked him for his concern and departed. The camera followed this couple to their old car, and eavesdropped as they bowed their heads and recommitted themselves to the Lord. In the months that passed the man never lost his poise. Nor was he glib about his illness. He was not in denial. He simply had come to terms with the cancer and its probable outcome. He knew the Lord was in control, and he refused to be shaken in his faith.

The cameras were present on his last Sunday in church, when he stood to speak. He said, 'Some of you have asked me if I'm mad at God for this disease that has taken over my body. I'll tell you honestly that I have nothing but love in my heart for my Lord. He didn't do this to me. We live in a sinful world where sickness and death are the curse man has brought upon himself. And I'm going to a better place where there will be no more tears, no suffering and no heartache. So don't feel bad for me . . . '

Then, this frail black man began to sing unaccompanied. He sang about his confidence in God and the better life ahead for him.

> **Themes:** Anger, Bitterness, Confidence – in God, Death, Fallen creation, Heaven, Hope, Love – for God, Love – God's, Marriage, Pain, Peace, Prayer, Recommitment, Relationships, Shock, Suffering.

> **Scriptures:** Matthew 5:12; John 1:2–4; 14:6; Romans 4:18; 5:1–5; 5:2; 8:8–25; 12:12; 15:13; 1 Corinthians 13:13; 15:19; 2 Corinthians 1:10; 4:17; Galatians 5:5–6; Ephesians 1:8; 2:12; 4:4; Colossians 1:5, 27; 3:4; 1 Thessalonians 1:2–3; 4:13; 5:3; Hebrews 3:6; 6:10–12; 10:36; 13:14; 1 Peter 1:3–9, 13, 21; 2 Peter 1:3–21; 2:9; 1 John 2:28; 3:2.

17: Change

Søren Kierkegaard was a Danish theologian who lived from 1813 to 1855. He related a homely parable about a flock of geese that milled around in a filthy barnyard imprisoned by a high wooden fence.

One day a preaching goose came into their midst. He stood on an old crate and admonished the geese for being content with this confined, earthbound existence. He recounted the exploits of their forefathers who spread their wings and flew trackless wastes of the sky. He spoke of the goodness of the Creator who had given geese the urge to migrate and the wings to fly. This pleased the geese. They nodded their heads and marvelled at these things and applauded the eloquence of the preaching goose. All this they did. But one thing they never did; they did not fly. They went back to their waiting dinner, for the corn was good and the barnyard secure.

Themes: Courage, Discipleship, Fear, Following, Leadership, Parables, Parable – Two Houses, Parable – Ten Virgins, Preaching, Purpose, Vision.

Scriptures: Exodus 15:22–27; 16:1–3; 17:1–8; Matthew 7:21–27; 25:1–13; Romans 2:13; James 1:22–24.

18: *Christian living*

On 28 May 1972 the Duke of Windsor, the uncrowned King Edward VIII, died in Paris. The same evening a television programme rehearsed the main events of his life. Extracts from earlier films were shown, in which he answered questions about his upbringing, brief reign and abdication. Recalling his boyhood as Prince of Wales, he said: 'My father (King George V) was a strict disciplinarian. Sometimes when I had done something wrong, he would admonish me saying, "My dear boy, you must always remember who you are".'

Themes: Children of God, Discipline, Parenting, Holiness, Sanctification, Sons of God, Sonship.

Scriptures: Leviticus 19:2; Deuteronomy 14:1–2; Proverbs 22:6; Isaiah 29:13; Jeremiah 31:9; Hosea 11:1; Joel 2:12–13; Matthew 15:19–20; John 1:12; Romans 6:1–6, 11, 19; 8:14–17; 2 Corinthians 6:16; 7:1; Galatians 2:20; 4:4–7; 5:16–26; Ephesians 1:5; 2:10; 4:1; 5:3–5; Colossians 1:10; 3:12–17; 1 Thessalonians 4:1; 1 Timothy 2:15; 2 Timothy 2:21; Titus 2:13; 3:1; Hebrews 12:10, 14; 1 Peter 1:15–16; 2:12, 15; 4:2; 3 John 11.

19: Christmas

At Christmas 1971 John McCain's peace was broken and mended. His Navy plane had been shot down over Hanoi during the Vietnam war. For five-and-a-half years he was to be a prisoner. On this particular Christmas Eve, John and two dozen other freezing prisoners huddled together to celebrate Christmas in their tattered clothes. For some of the men, who had been in isolation, it was the first time they had been together for seven years. Physically, they were skin and bone; mere shadows of their former selves. Some were too weak or too sick to stand. But, their frail and croaky voices gladly forced out the carol:

> Hark! The herald angels sing
> glory to the newborn king,
> peace on earth, . . .

At one point, they even exchanged imaginary gifts they had pretended to collect from the barren prison cell. John read brief snatches of the Christmas story he had been able to scribble down on a piece of paper earlier when they were given a Bible for only a few minutes.

'An angel said to them,' John read out, "Fear not: for, behold, I bring you good tidings . . . "

Yet, tears were rolling down their unshaven faces as memories were refreshed of the time – almost a year before – when North Vietnamese guards burst in on a church service some of them were attending.

The guards beat the three prisoners leading the prayers. The rest were locked away for the next eleven months in cells not quite one metre by two metres in size. But now they could sing their favourite carol, *Silent Night*.

Some years later John McCain recalled; 'We had forgotten our wounds, our hunger, our pain . . . There was an absolutely exquisite feeling that all our burdens had been lifted . . . The Vietnamese guards did not disturb us. But as I looked up at the barred windows, I wished they had been looking in. I *wanted* them to see us, joyful and, yes, triumphant.'

Themes: Enemies – love of, Fear, Gifts, Joy, Peace, Prison, Suffering, Triumphant, War.

Scriptures: Leviticus 19:18; Deuteronomy 32:35; Psalms 27:14; 34:14; Proverbs 20:22; Isaiah 9:6; Daniel 3:16–18; Matthew 5:22–24, 43–48; Luke 2:10, 14; 6:27–36; 10:20, 27; 23:34; John 14:1–4; 15:11; 16:33; Acts 7:60; Romans 5:1–5; 12:9–21; 1 Corinthians 7:15; 13; 2 Corinthians 11:30; 12:9; Galatians 6:2; Ephesians 1:9; Philippians 4:6–7, 13;1 Thessalonians 5:13; 2 Timothy 2:22; Hebrews 10:30, 36; James 1:2; 1 Peter 3:9, 11.

20: Comfort

A mother sent her daughter to the corner shop to buy some milk. It was to be the little girl's first such trip on her own. The mother made it plain her little girl should go straight to the shop and then come straight home. However, the girl was away two hours. Her mother was almost beside herself with worry. When her daughter arrived home she tore strips off her, 'Where have you been?'

The girl was quick to answer, 'I'm so sorry Mum. I know I am late. But Jane broke her doll and I had to stop and help her fix it.'

But the mother replied, 'And how could you help her fix that broken doll?'

The girl's response was innocent, 'I really couldn't, but I sat down with her and helped her cry.'

Themes: Burden, Encouragement, Funerals, Grief, Love – of neighbour, Suffering, Sympathy.

Scriptures: John 11:19; Acts 11:22–26; 15:41; Romans 14:19; 15:1; 1 Corinthians 10:23; 2 Corinthians 1:3–7; Galatians 6:2; Ephesians 4:29; 6:2; Colossians 4:8; 1 Thessalonians 3:2; 4:18; 5:11, 14; 2 Thessalonians 2:16–17; James 2:8.

21: Commitment

For many years Admiral Hyman Rickover was the head of the United State Nuclear Navy. His admirers and his critics held strongly opposing views about the stern and demanding Admiral. For many years every officer aboard a nuclear submarine was personally interviewed and approved by Rickover. Those who went through those interviews usually came out shaking with fear, anger or total intimidation. Among them was Ex-President Jimmy Carter who, years ago, applied for service under Rickover. This is his account of a Rickover interview:

I had applied for the Nuclear Submarine Program, and Admiral Rickover was interviewing me for the job. It was the first time I met Admiral Rickover, and we sat in a large room by ourselves for more than two hours, and he let me choose any subjects I wished to discuss. Very carefully, I chose those about which I knew most at the time – current events, seamanship, music, literature, naval tactics, electronics, gunnery – and he began to ask me a series of questions of increasing difficulty. In each instance, he soon proved that I knew relatively little about the subject I had chosen.

He always looked right into my eyes, and he never smiled. I was saturated with cold sweat.

Finally, he asked a question and I thought I could redeem myself. He said, 'How did you stand in your class at the Naval Academy?' Since I had completed my Sophomore year at Georgia Tech before entering Annapolis as a Pleb, I had done very well and I swelled my chest with pride and answered 'Sir, I stood fifty-ninth in a class of 820!' I sat back to wait for the congratulations – which never came. Instead the question came 'Did you do your best?' I started to say, 'Yes, sir', but I remembered who this was and recalled several of the many times at the Academy when I could have learned more about our allies, our enemies, weapons, strategy, and so forth. I was just human. I finally gulped and said, 'No, sir, I didn't always do my best.'

He looked at me for a long time, and then turned his chair around to end the interview. He asked one final question, which I have never been able to forget – or to answer. He said, 'Why not?' I sat there for a while shaken, and then slowly left the room.

Themes: Achievement, Ethics, Failure, Following, Leadership, Parable – of the Talents, Perseverance, Success, Work, Zeal.

Scriptures: Matthew 16:27; 25:14–30; Acts 22:3; Romans 12:11; 13:13; 14:7–8; 1 Corinthians 4:1–2; 14:12; Galatians 4:18; 5:13; 6:9; Ephesians 4:28; 6:5–9; Colossians 1:10; 3:23–24; 1 Thessalonians 4:11; 2 Thessalonians 2:16–17; 3:10; 1 Timothy 4:11–13; 2 Timothy 2:21; Titus 2:14; 1 Peter 4:10.

22: Communication

In the days of the wild west, a lone cowboy went riding and came upon an Indian lying motionless on the road. His right ear was pressed to the ground. He was muttering soberly to himself. 'Stage coach! Three people inside. Two men, one woman. Four horses. Three dappled grey, one black. Stage coach moving west.'

The cowboy was amazed. 'Say, that's incredible

pardner! You can tell all that just by listening to the ground?'

'No,' said the Indian. 'Stage coach run over me thirty minutes ago.'

Themes: Humour, Knowledge – gift of, Prophecy, Revelation – gift of.

Scriptures: Romans 12:6; 1 Corinthians 12:8, 10, 28; 13:2, 8; 14:6, 30; Ephesians 4:11; 1 Thessalonians 5:20.

23: Cross

It was May 21, 1946. The place was Los Alamos. A young and daring scientist was carrying out a necessary experiment in preparation for the atomic test to be conducted in the waters of the South Pacific atoll at Bikini.

He had successfully performed such an experiment many times before. In his effort to determine the amount of U-235 necessary for a chain reaction – scientists call it the critical mass – he would push two hemispheres of uranium together. Then, just as the mass became critical, he would push them apart with his screwdriver, thus instantly stopping the chain reaction.

But that day, just as the material became critical, the screwdriver slipped! The hemispheres of uranium came too close together. Instantly the room was filled with a dazzling bluish haze. Young Louis Slotin, instead of ducking and thereby possibly saving himself, tore the two hemispheres apart with his hands and thus interrupted the chain reaction.

By this instant, self-forgetful daring, he saved the lives of the seven other persons in the room. As he waited for the car that was to take them to the hospital, he said quietly to his companion, 'You'll come through all right, but I haven't the faintest chance myself.' It was only too true. Nine days later he died in agony.

Themes: Courage, Easter, Jesus – his death, Jesus – his work, Ransom, Representative man, Sacrifice, Substitution, Suffering.

Scriptures: Mark 10:45; 15:21–37; Luke 24:21; John 1:29; 1 Corinthians 1:30; 5:7; Galatians 3:13; Ephesians 1:7; Titus 2:14; Hebrews 5:8–10; 13:12; 1 Peter 1:18–19; 2:21; 3:18; 4:1.

24: Discoveries

In 1847 Sir James Simpson was a doctor in Edinburgh when he discovered chloroform, one of the most significant discoveries in modern medicine. Some years later after a lecture a student asked him, 'What do you consider to be the most valuable discovery of your lifetime?' He answered, 'My most valuable discovery was when I discovered myself a sinner and that Jesus Christ was my Saviour.'

Themes: Forgiveness, Humility, Parable – Pearl of Great Price, Sin.

Scriptures: Matthew 13:14; Luke 14:33; Philippians 3:7–9; I Timothy 1:15; 2 Peter 1:3.

25: *Distractions*

An Eastern Air Lines jumbo jet took off from New York's John F Kennedy Airport. It was 9.20pm on 29 December, 1972. The plane was headed for Miami in Florida. On board were 163 passengers and thirteen crew members. Like almost every other plane flight the journey was uneventful. That is, until the approach to Miami Airport. The landing gear handle was placed in the 'down' position, but the green light, which would have indicated that the nose landing gear was fully extended, failed to illuminate.

At 11.31pm the Captain called the control tower to report his problem. The control tower advised the captain to climb back to 2,000 feet. The plane then circled over the desolate, marshy, Florida Everglades. The captain instructed the first officer to engage the automatic pilot. The first officer was then free to repair the nose gear light. He successfully removed the light lens assembly. But it jammed when he attempted to replace it. He continued to have difficulty.

The captain asked the second officer to go down into the electronics bay to see if the landing gear had gone into place. But it was too dark down there. The second officer climbed back into the cockpit and said he could not tell whether or not the nose wheel was up or down. So the crew continued its attempt to free the nose gear light lens from its retainer.

In the midst of all this, a half-second musical C-chord sounded in the cockpit. This was indicating a deviation of 250 feet from the selected altitude. No crew memeber commented on the chime.

The controller in the tower noticed his radar showing the jumbo at only 900 feet. So he asked how things were coming along. The cockpit voice recorder recorded that the reply was, 'Okay, we'd like to turn around and come back in'. At 11.42pm the plane was turned with its left wing lowered.

Suddenly the captain said, 'Hey, what's happened here?' At 11.42 and 10 seconds the altimeter warning beeps persistently sounded in the cockpit. The captain and the first officer frantically tried to pour on the power. They pulled back on the controls. Unfortunately, it takes from one to six seconds for jet engines to develop thrust.

Two seconds later, with the aircraft in the left bank, Flight 401 ploughed into the desolate Evergades. The plane disintegrated. One hundred and one people had been killed because highly-paid pilots fiddled with a seventy-five cent light bulb. Miraculously, seventy-five people survived.

Themes: Commitment, Discipleship, False leaders, Guidance, Leadership, Priorities, Tragedy.

Scriptures: Mark 13:22; 1 Corinthians 7:35; Galatians 6:9; 2 Peter 2:1; 1 John 4:1.

26: Encouragement

Nicholas Young was not even a teenager when he joined Captain James Cook's boat *Endeavour* in 1768 as 'the surgeon's boy'.

On 26 August he was one of nearly a hundred men on the ship when it sailed quietly out of Plymouth Harbour. They were heading for Tahiti to observe the transit of Venus on 3 June the following year.

With the task completed Cook left Tahiti. He sailed south looking for the unknown continent. He found no sign of it. He gave up and turned west in search of New Zealand.

After much patience, by mid-September there were signs of land: seaweed floating by, one or two pieces of barnacle-covered wood and a seal asleep in the water (seals don't venture far from land). Expectations were rising.

To encourage the vigilance of his crew, Cook promised a gallon of rum to the first person to sight land, with the further promise that his name should be given to some part of the coast.

It was Saturday, 7 October. The twelve-year-old Nicholas was up the mast in the gentle easterly breezes carrying the ship along. At 2pm young Nick, as he was called, sighted land and gave the excited cry.

True to his promise, and as a way of encouraging his crew, Cook named the south-west point of Poverty Bay, 'Young Nick's Head'.

Themes: Barnabas, Leadership.

Scriptures: Acts 11:22–26; 15:41; Romans 14:19; 1 Corinthians 10:23; Ephesians 4:29; 1 Thessalonians 5:11.

27: Evangelism

In a meeting of pastors in Australia Ed Silvoso told the following story. The mayor of the city of Resistencia in Argentina invited Ed to his office. The mayor, who was a colonel in the army, had heard about Ed through his radio station and a Christian newspaper. He asked if Ed's organization could help build water tanks for twenty-one neighbourhoods that had no running water. During the discussion the mayor brought in the engineer and the drawings. Eventually, as they were parting, Ed asked if he could pray for him. The big macho mayor said, 'Sure, go for it!' So Ed prayed, and the power of God came over him. He was so moved that tears came to the rim of his eyes.

The next day the mayor turned up unannounced at a pastor's luncheon. He said, 'Silvoso, whatever I got yesterday, I love it and I came here for seconds.' Ed invited him to sit down next to him and began to share the good news of Jesus with him. Then he said, 'Can I pray for you?'

'*Please*! Go for it'. Ed said he did not have this effect on people, but he had to hold up the mayor as he prayed. He was ready to hit the floor.

Eventually, Ed's organization finished erecting the first two water tanks. The mayor rang and asked if Ed could bless them.

'You provide the microphone and I will bring a Bible. That's all I need and I will bless the water tanks,' Ed replied. In passing, Ed asked if a little plaque could be put by the tap on the tank. On the plaque he asked for the words from John's Gospel where Jesus says, 'Whoever drinks of this water shall thirst again, but if they drink of the water I give them, they will never thirst again.'

On the day of the blessing, when the car was about 100 metres away the quotation could be read with ease. Rather than a plaque, the mayor had hired a professional painter. With the colours of the Argentine flag, the entire face of the water tank was covered with the Bible verse. The politicians and other officials made their speeches. In the end they said, 'Okay Reverend, would you bless the water tank?' Ed stood up and said, 'Would you turn with me to the water tank and read?' And they all read from the water tank. Ed spoke briefly on the text on the tank, and then gave an invitation and many people received Christ, including the mayor.

Themes: Power encounter, Prayer, Preaching, Servant evangelism.

Scriptures: John 4:13–14; Acts 17:22–33; Romans 14:19; 1 Thessalonians 1:5.

28: *Evangelism*

In one of his conferences, Ed Silvoso told the story of Olmos Prison in the city of La Plata, south-east of Buenos Aires. A few years ago, this prison of 2,700 inmates – Argentina's largest maximum security prison – was totally out of control. There was not a single Christian on the premises. There was male prostitution, extortion, murder and riots. Mafia bosses, drug dealers and gangsters had the run of the place. There was so much evil that there was even a church of Satan operating daily. There were animal sacrifices on a weekly basis. Some people even reported that demons materialized and walked around.

In the city nearby, a pastor committed a crime and was sentenced to serve time in the gaol. The pastor repented and cried out to God, 'O God, would you give me a second chance and fill me with your Holy Spirit?' The Lord forgave him and filled him with the Spirit. Now the pastor had nothing to lose. He became a 'spiritual kamikaze'. He began to drive himself into the church of Satan and into the Mafia circles and among the gangsters to share the good news of Jesus with tremendous boldness.

At the same time as this was happening, another pastor applied for a job in the prison. The place was so evil that all three officials who interviewed him each told him basically the same thing, 'We don't want you here. We hate you, and if you get this job we will kill you.' But he got the job.

Now, with one Christian in the cells and one Christian in the administration they began to pray. One of the first things they prayed for was time on the prison radio. Eventually they got an hour-and-a-half a week. That may not sound like much. But this radio station broadcasts to a captive audience. You cannot move the dial, you cannot turn down the volume, you cannot throw out the speakers. As these two men prayed, and as the gospel was pumped in, men came to the Lord.

Then persecution of the Christians began. However, the Christians discovered they could apply for protection under the constitution. The gaol had five stories and was organized into cell blocks of forty-two inmates. The Christians said, 'We need a cell block of our own so that all we Christians can be together.' They were given the very worst cell block on the fourth floor. The church of Satan, the Mafia, the gangsters and the drug dealers lived there. Nevertheless, the Christians moved in and formed a church. They recognised a pastor and set aside elders. Then they divided themselves into seven teams of six men. One team was to be on duty each night from 11.00pm to 5.00am. Two read the Bible, two prayed, and the other two went from bed to bed, laying hands on their fellow inmates, and interceding before God to bless them and their relations on the outside. After two hours the pairs would switch roles. They did such an excellent job that today over 1,500 of the inmates are born again Christians.

Themes: Church growth, Demons, Elders, Evil, Forgiveness, Guidance, Intercession, Leadership, Persecution, Prayer, Prayer vigils, Principalities and powers, Spiritual warfare.

Scriptures: Genesis 37:22–24; 39:19–23; 40:1–8; 42:16–19; 50:19–20; Exodus 18; Judges 16:21–25; 1 Kings 22:27; 2 Chronicles 16:10; 18:26; Isaiah 42:7; Jeremiah 32:2, 8, 12; 33:1; 37:16, 20, 21; 38:6, 13, 28; Acts 14:23; 16:23–40; 21:27–22:29, 28:30; Romans 8:28, 38; 1 Corinthians 15:24; 2 Corinthians 6:5; 11:23; Ephesians 1:20–21; 2:10; 3:8–10; 4:11–12; 6:20; Philippians 1:7, 13, 14, 16, 17; Colossians 2:9–10, 15; 4:3, 18; 2 Timothy 1:16; 2:9; Philemon 10, 13.

29: Evangelism – power

John Wimber says that it was at the end of a long day of ministry. He was exhausted and was looking forward to relaxing on the plane journey home. Shortly after take-off he pushed back the seat. As he glanced around he saw something that startled him. Across the aisle was a middle-aged business man. What Wimber could see written across his face was the word 'adultery'. He blinked and rubbed his eyes, but was still seeing the word 'adultery'. It was not with his natural eyes but in his mind's eye that he could see this word. By now the man had become aware that John was looking at him.

'What do you want?' he snapped. As the man spoke, a woman's name came clearly to John's mind.

Somewhat nervously, John leaned across the aisle and asked, 'Does the name Jane (not her real name) mean anything to you?'

The poor fellow's face turned ashen. 'We've got to talk,' he stammered.

They went off to the upstairs lounge of the plane. As John followed him up the stairs he sensed the Spirit speaking to him again. 'Tell him if he doesn't turn from his adultery, I'm going to take him'. Terrific. All John wanted was a nice quiet plane ride. But, here was John sitting in an aeroplane cocktail lounge with a man he had never seen before, whose name he didn't even know, about to tell him God was going to take his life if he didn't stop his affair with some woman.

They sat down in strained silence. The man looked at John suspiciously for a moment. Then he asked, 'Who told you that name?'

'God told me,' John blurted out. He was too rattled to think of a better way to put it.

'*God* told you?' he almost shouted back.

'Yes. He also told me to tell you . . . that unless you turn from this adulterous relationship, he is going to take your life.'

John braced himself for the angry defence. But instead the man crumbled and his heart melted. In a choked desperate voice he asked John, 'What should I do?'

John explained what it meant to repent or turn away from what is wrong in our lives and to trust Christ with our lives. Then John began to lead the man in a quiet prayer. But the man exploded.

Bursting into tears he cried out, 'O *God*, I'm so *sorry* . . . ' And the man launched into the most heart-rending repentance John had ever heard.

It was impossible to hide what was happening. Before long every one in the tiny cocktail lounge was intimately acquainted with this man's past, and now his present contrition. Even the stewardess was weeping along with him.

When things had calmed down the man explained why he was so upset by the mention of the name Jane. His wife was sitting right next to him.

And then John said, 'You're going to have to tell her.'

'I am? When?' he responded weakly.

'Better do it right now,' was John's suggestion.

So off they went downstairs. John couldn't hear the conversation over the noise of the plane. But he could see the stunned look on the wife's face. Her eyes were wide. She stared first at her husband and then at John and then back again. In the end the man led his wife to Christ, there and then.

The plane landed and there was little time to talk. They didn't have a Bible. John gave them his and they went their separate ways.

Themes: Adultery, Confession, Conversion, Forgiveness, Guilt, Knowledge – gift of, Repentance, Sin.

Scriptures: Exodus 20:14; 32:14; Leviticus 5:5; 16:21; 18:20; 26:40–42; Numbers 5:5–7; Deuteronomy 5:18; 22:22–24; 32:36; Judges 2:18; 1 Kings 8:33–34; 1 Chronicles 21:16; 2 Chronicles 7:14; Nehemiah 1:6; 9:2, 17; Psalms 32:5; 51; 106:45; 135:14; Proverbs 28:13; Jeremiah 18:8; 26:3, 13, 19; 42:10; Daniel 9:9, 20; Joel 2:13–14; Jonah 4:2; Matthew 3:6; 18:21–35; Mark 1:15; 2:1–12; 10:11; 11:25; Luke 3:7–14; John 8:1–11, 31–36; Acts 2:38; 17:30; 19:18; 26:20; Romans 3:23; 6:23; 12:6; 13:9; 1 Corinthians 12:10; Galatians 5:19; Ephesians 4:32; Colossians 2:13; Hebrews 1; James 2:11; 5:16; 1 John 1:9; 2:12.

30: Evangelism – presence

A Christian went to China and saw the pastor of a fast-growing Baptist church. The man from the west asked how he went about evangelism. The answer was a surprise. The Chinese Christian said this quite naturally, 'I don't do much searching out of people. They come to me!' The reason became obvious. During the Cultural Revolution (1966–68) this man had been conscripted to work in a soul-destroying factory. He was making parts for radios. He was not allowed to speak about Christ at all. But he whistled while he worked. That was significant, for nobody else in that factory could summon up the joy to whistle.

When the days of the cultural revolution were over, the man returned to his work as a pastor. Now there was a steady trickle of people from the factory knocking at his office door. They wanted to find out what was the secret of his joy. It if could carry him serenely through such unpleasant circumstances, it must be worth hearing about.

Themes: Fruit of the Spirit, Joy, Suffering, Work.

Scriptures: Nehemiah 8:10; Matthew 25:14–30; Luke 2:10; 6:20–22; 19:11–27; John 17:13; Acts 2:46; 27:22, 25; Romans 12:11; 13:13, 1 Corinthians 4:2; 2 Corinthians 4:7–18; 6:4–10; 11:23–28; Galatians 4:18; 5:22; 6:9; Ephesians 4:28; 6:5–9; Colossians 1:10; 3:23–24; 1 Thessalonians 4:11; 1 Timothy 4:12; Titus 2:14; James 1:25; 1 Peter 3:14; 4:13–14; 1 John 1:4; Revelation 22:14.

31: Evil

A horrific example of evil comes from the testimony of S Szmaglewska, a Polish guard at the Nuremberg War Crimes Tribunal. As a witness he said:

> . . . women carrying children were (always) sent with them to the crematorium. [Children were of no labour value so they were killed. The mothers were sent along, too, because separation might lead to panic and hysteria, which might slow up the destruction process, and this could not be afforded. It was simpler to condemn the mothers too and

keep things quiet and smooth.] The children were then torn from their parents outside the crematorium and sent to the gas chambers separately. [At that point, crowding more people into the gas chambers became the most urgent consideration. Separately meant that more children could be packed in separately, or they could be thrown in over the heads of the adults once the chambers were packed.] When the extermination of the Jews in the gas chambers was at its height, orders were issued that children were to be thrown straight into the crematorium furnaces, or into a pit near the crematorium, without being gassed first.

Smirnov (Russian prosecutor) How am I to understand this? Did they throw them into the fire alive, or did they kill them first?

Witness They threw them in alive. Their screams could be heard in the camp. It is difficult to say how many children were killed in this way.

Smirnov Why did they do this?

Witness It is very difficult to say. We don't know whether they wanted to economize on gas, or if it was because there was not enough room in the gas chambers.

Themes: Cross, Crucifixion, Holocaust, Murder, Suffering, Tragedy, War.

Scriptures: Job; Psalms 91; 118:5–6; Matthew 5:4; Mark 11:22–24; 15:21–39; Luke 7:1–10; 8:22–25; 10:27; 2 Corinthians 1:3–11; James 1:2; 1 Peter 1:6; 5:10.

32: Evil

Up until 1973, London's fruit and veg market occupied the square at Covent Garden. In times past they used to sell caged nightingales. Nightingales were known for their beautiful song. Sadly, the birds were captured and blinded by inserting hot needles into their eyes. Because nightingales sing in the dark, a liquid song bubbled almost endlessly from the caged and blinded birds. People had enslaved and blinded the birds to gratify their own desires. More than this, the birds had been enslaved in such a way they could never enjoy freedom. No one could set them free.

Themes: Eschatology, Freedom, Joy, Slavery, Suffering.

Scriptures: Nehemiah 8:10; Job; Isaiah 61:1; Luke 2:10; 4:18; 6:20–22; John 17:13; Acts 2:46; 27:22, 25; Romans 1:1; 8:21; 1 Corinthians 7:22; 9:19, 22–23; 2 Corinthians 3:17; Galatians 3:24; 5:1, 22; James 1:2–4, 25; 1 Peter 2:16; 3:14; 4:13–14; 1 John 1:4; Revelation 22:14.

33: Examinations

A student was to sit for his final exams in logic. He was doing philosophy at college. The exam was particularly difficult. It was not an open book exam but the lecturer had said they could bring as much information into the exam room as they could fit on an A4 sheet of paper.

On the day of the examination students came with their crammed pieces of paper. But one student came with a completely blank sheet of paper. Seating himself for the examination, the student put his piece of paper on the floor. He had also brought with him a friend who was an advanced student in logic. He got his friend to stand on the piece of paper. The advanced student told him all he needed to know for the exam. He was the only student to receive an 'A'.

Themes: College, Gifts, Grace, Humour, Students, Works of the law.

Scriptures: Romans 3:19–31; Galatians 2:16; Ephesians 2:1–10; Titus 3:1–11.

34: Exorcism

One day John Tunstall, a minister, received an emergency phone call from a woman in his new church. The woman was in a panic and John could hear strange voices in the background. When he arrived at her house, the woman was slouched in a chair staring at him. In a masculine voice she said, 'You are the man of God? I have been waiting for you. Show me your power!'

John had come to expect that God would work powerfully. So he snapped back at the spirit, 'Show me *your* power!'

Instantly, a flowerpot on a shelf exploded into pieces

with a loud noise. But John was ready for it. He said, 'My power is the blood of the Lord Jesus Christ. In Jesus' name I command you to leave that woman.' The evil spirit struggled and the woman slithered onto the floor like a snake, then writhed around. But the power of Jesus prevailed, the demon left, and the woman was completely well.

Themes: Deliverance, Demonic, Demons, Evil Spirits, God – his power, Healing, Jesus – his name, Medicine, Psychiatry, Spirits, Suffering.

Scriptures: Psalm 34; Mark 1:21–28; 5:1–20; 7:24–30; 9:14–29; Acts 16:16–18; 19:11–20.

35: Exorcism

A woman, whom we will call Judy, was the 28-year-old wife of a missionary from Europe. Soon after arriving home she complained to her husband about seeing strange and twisted faces over her own face when she gazed into windows at night. She also told of having terrifying dreams, something that started in France after she prayed for a man who had claimed to have demonic problems. Judy also had other problems that had been lifelong struggles for her. For example, as long as she could remember she had been infatuated with married men about whom she had sexual fantasies. Soon after she arrived back from the mission field she was in a small

Christian meeting and behaved in a bizarre manner. For no apparent reason, she cried out, fell to the floor and began thrashing around. The wife of the leader of the meeting approached Judy.

In a voice that did not seem her own Judy said, 'I hate you.'

Blaine, the group leader, then picked up Judy in order to take her to another room for prayer. On the way Judy hit him in the mouth. During the prayer time the Holy Spirit helped to identify demons or evil spiritual beings causing trouble in Judy's life.

Blaine put his hand on her head and said, 'You demons of defiance, adultery, anger and fear, be gone from this child of God.'

As Blaine prayed, Judy fell to the ground. Then she experienced immediate and dramatic relief from her oppression. Since then she has had no problems with habitual sexual fantasies, or demonic dreams or seeing evil spirits on her face. For a short time she continued to have a problem with anger. But the problem gradually went away as she continued to meet with Blaine and a small group for counselling, prayer and encouragement. Today Judy is back in Europe serving the Lord as a missionary.

Themes: Deliverance, Demonic, Demons, Evil Spirits, God – his power, Healing, Jesus – his name, Medicine, Psychiatry, Spirits, Suffering.

Scriptures: Psalm 34; Mark 1:21–28; 5:1–20; 7:24–30; 9:14–29; Acts 16:16–18; 19:11–20.

36: Faith

Sarah is seventeen. When she was thirteen she got something like the flu. But then her eyesight began to degenerate. Her memory started to go. Tests were done at the hospital, but they could find nothing wrong.

As the months passed, Sarah lost more and more muscle control as well as mental ability. At the beginning of 1994 she was transferred to a special hospital for chronic care.

On 27 February 1994, Sarah's friend Rachel went to church. She was prayed for in the ministry time. She had a vision and sensed God saying that she needed to go to the hospital to pray for Sarah.

The next day, Rachel and her dad went to the hospital to pray for Sarah. Sarah was in a special wheelchair that looked more like a bed. Saliva was dribbling out of her mouth. She could hear voices but could not see or comprehend what was going on. Rachel and Simon wheeled Sarah to a quiet spot in the hospital.

They began to pray for her. As they prayed over the next two-and-a-half hours, Sarah began to cry and then to shake. Her sight began to come back. Her legs started to move. Slowly she began to sit up on her own. The dribbling stopped. Eventually she was able to say, 'I'm getting stronger.'

Before coming into the hospital Rachel was so convinced Jesus was going to heal Sarah that she had brought some potato chips for her to eat. Over the next few days, Sarah began walking and eating those chips. Her sight began to improve. News of what was happening spread quickly through the hospital.

On 22 April 1994, Sarah returned home from the chronic care hospital.

Themes: Guidance, Healing, Knowledge – gift of, Miracles, Prayer, Trust, Visions.

Scriptures: Deuteronomy 32:20; Psalms 18:2; 26:1; 37:3–6; Proverbs 3:5; Mark 2:1–12; 5:21–43, 36; 9:14–29; 10:46–52; 11:20–24; Luke 17:6; John 4:48; 5:1–9; 10:38; 20:30–31; Acts 4:30; 14:9; 1 Corinthians 12:8, 9, 28, 30; 13:2, 8; 14:6, 30; Hebrews 2:4

37: Faith

John Paton, the pioneer missionary to the New Hebrides, was translating the Scriptures into the language of the people of the southern seas. He had great difficulty in securing a word for faith for there seemed to be no equivalent in their language. He made it a matter of special prayer. One day one of his workers came in from a hard day's work, and leaned back in a lounge chair and said, 'Oh, I am so tired I feel I must lean my whole weight on this chair.'

'Praise God,' said Paton, 'I've got my word. "God so loved the world that he gave his only begotten Son, that whosoever leaneth his whole weight on him shall not perish, but have everlasting life".'

Themes: Bible, God – his care, Guidance, Missionaries, Prayer, Trust.

Scriptures: Psalms 18:2; 26:1; 37:3–6; Proverbs 3:5; Matthew 11:29; Mark 2:1–12; 5:21–43; 9:14–29; 10:46–52; 11:20–24; Luke 17:6; John 3;16; 4:48; 5:1–9; 10:38; 20:30–31; Acts 14:9.

38: Faithfulness

Richard Wurmbrandt was a Romanian pastor. When he and his wife were thrown into prison by Communists, their nine-year-old son was hauled off to a government school to be indoctrinated in Marxism and atheism.

Some years later, as a method of psychological torture for his parents, the boy was brought to see his mother. The purpose of the visit was the denouncing of Christianity to her face. He studied the marks of suffering written on his mother's face together with the joy evident in his mother's spirit. The son suddenly declared, 'Mother, if Christ means this much to you, then I want him too.'

Themes: Example, Joy, Parents, Persecution, Prison, Suffering, Witnessing.

Scriptures: Job; Matthew 5:12; Acts 5:41; 9:4–5; 14:22; Romans 5:3; 8:17–18; 12:12; 1 Corinthians 12:26–27; 2 Corinthians 1:3–7; Philippians 1:29; 3:10; 1 Thessalonians 1:6; 2 Timothy 3:12; Hebrews 2:18; 4:15; 12:3, 5, 11; 13:13; James 1:2–14; 1 Peter 1:6–7; 2:21; 4:1–2, 12–16; 5:9.

39: Families

A thirty-two-year-old woman rang a Christian psychiatrist's office. When she was told that she could not be seen for two months she began to scream and cry. The secretary handed the phone to the psychiatrist. The lady said she did not think she could survive any longer as she was. It turned out she could be seen.

At the appointment the lady said that she was raised in a religious home, but her mother had used love withdrawal as a way of disciplining her, by refusing to speak to her and turning her back on her for up to two weeks at a time.

To get away from the verbal abuse of this so-called 'Christian' mother, she married in her second year at college. Her husband was a successful man, but he was also a bore, as she put it. After their first child she had an affair. The same thing happened after the second child. A few months later she moved in with another man. Then she began dating a biker. He introduced her to shop lifting, drugs and Satan worship. At this very first visit the psychiatrist introduced her to Christ. After accepting Christ, the woman announced, 'I'm free, I feel as though a burden has been lifted.'

She went home and within a few days again felt oppressed. But then she burnt her books on witchcraft and Satan and was relieved. She then planned to return to her husband.

Themes: Abuse, Children, Conversion, Discipline, Healing – inner, Love, Parenting, Religion.

Scriptures: Deuteronomy 6:20–25; Matthew 5:21–26; Romans 12:10, 16–18; Ephesians 6:1–4; Colossians 3:18–21

40: Fathers

A father was waiting for his son to go to gaol. A friend said to the man, 'I hear that lad of yours has been in trouble again.'

'I am afraid he has,' said the father.

'Ah!' said the other fellow, 'I know it is not the first time by any means. I know all you've tried to do for him in the past. But I gather the offence is worse than ever this time. Do you know what I would do if he was my son? I'd put him smartly out the door, shut it, and then turn the key once and for all.'

'Aye,' said the father, 'do you know, if he were a lad of yours I would do exactly the same thing. But you see he is my son and I will not.'

Themes: Acceptance, Children, Families, Forgiveness, Love, Parable – Prodigal Son, Parenting, Prison, Rejection, Sin.

Scriptures: Deuteronomy 6:20–25; Matthew 5:21–26; Romans 12:10, 16–18; 15:11–32; Ephesians 6:1–4; Colossians 3:18–21.

41: Forgiveness

Erich Honeker was the head of government in former East Germany. In the downfall of the Communist regime (1989–90), Honeker and Margot, his wife, were evicted from their luxurious palace in Vandlitz and made homeless.

For twenty-six years Mrs Honeker had been responsible for education policy. Anyone who refused to take an oath of atheistic allegiance to the state was refused higher education for their children.

Uwe Holmer, a Lutheran evangelical pastor and his wife had ten children, nine of whom had been refused higher education. Yet they took the Honekers into their home for two months, sharing their lives and meals with them.

As a result, the pastor and his wife were ostracised for harbouring a man who was so wicked, an 'enemy of the people'.

Themes: Acceptance, Martyrs, Parable – Unforgiving Servant, Rejection, Sacrifice, Shame.

Scriptures: 2 Samuel 11; Psalms 32; 51; Matthew 18:21–35; Mark 2:1–12; 11:25; Luke 6:27–38; 11:4; 17:3; Romans 12:14; 1 Corinthians 13; Galatians 6:2, 9.

42: Forgiveness

A minister's wife was having an affair. She wandered into the woods to think and pray through her broken and crumbling life. She poured out her bitterness to God and described her disastrous life to him. As she stood, silent and still before the Lord she had a vision. She saw a broken vessel representing her life. Into the picture came Jesus. Tenderly he stooped and sensitively picked up the broken pieces, as if every one was precious. With skill Jesus put the vessel together. In her vision the woman saw Jesus hold the flawless vessel up to her. That vision was a promise to the woman of the forgiveness and healing of Jesus, which enabled her to turn her back on the sin in her life and begin again in her marriage.

Themes: Adultery, Brokenness, Clergy, Healing – inner, Inner healing, Leadership, Recreation, Visions.

Scriptures: Exodus 34:6; 2 Samuel 11; Nehemiah 9:17; Psalms 32, 51; 103:12; Isaiah 38:17; 43:25; 61:1; Jeremiah 31:34; Daniel 9:9; Micah 7:19; Mark 2:1–12; Luke 4:18; John 8:1–11; Romans 3:25; 2 Corinthians 1:3–7; 1 John 1:9.

43: Forgiveness

A man not only embarrassed himself at a party, he positively humiliated his wife. The next day, looking to his wife for love he asked for her forgiveness. She readily agreed to forgive him. However, over the months ahead, whenever something came up that she didn't like, she would bring up the party incident. One day he said, 'I thought you forgave me for that.'

'Darling, I did,' she said. 'It's just that I don't want you to forget that I forgave you.'

Themes: Acceptance, Confession, Humour, Love, Marriage.

Scriptures: Exodus 34:6; Nehemiah 9:17; Psalm 103:12; Isaiah 38:17; 43:25; 61:1; Jeremiah 31:34; Daniel 9:9; Micah 7:19; Luke 4:18; James 5:16; 1 John 1:9.

44: Forgiveness

Stephen first learned about forgiveness from Miss Roberts, his first-grade teacher. Each day after lunch she allowed her class to purchase an 'orangesicle' – a frozen orange juice on a stick – for dessert. It was the highlight of Stephen's school day.

One day he forgot his money. It just so happened, however, that Miss Roberts had found a dime on the classroom floor that day and offered to return it to its owner. As he raced forward to claim the money, he was challenged by a red-haired girl who insisted that it was hers. Two people claiming the same dime – a problem for most people, but not for Miss Roberts. She settled the dispute quickly, suggesting that each of them bring a note from their mothers stating that they had been sent to school that day with a dime.

Miss Roberts must have seen the horror on Stephen's face, as he realized that everyone would soon discover that he was both a thief and a liar. He was already dreading the spanking his mother would give him for his dishonesty. Just as the consequences of his 'crime' were about to overwhelm him, Miss Roberts came and knelt beside his desk.

'Stevie, I found another dime,' she said. She looked him

right in the eye and handed the dime to him. 'Here, it must be yours.'

Immediately, Stephen broke down in tears and confessed what Miss Roberts already knew. 'That's OK,' she said, patting him on the head. 'We all make mistakes.' After apologizing to the red-haired girl, he enjoyed the best-tasting orangesicle he had ever eaten.

Themes: Atonement, Confession, Cross, Jesus – work of, Lord's Prayer, Solomon – widsom of, Wisdom.

Scriptures: Exodus 34:6; 2 Samuel 11–12; 1 Kings 3:16–28; Nehemiah 9:17; Psalms 32; 52; 103:12; Isaiah 38:17; 43:25; 61:1; Jeremiah 31:34; Daniel 9:9; Micah 7:19; Matthew 6:14–15; Mark 2:1–12; Luke 4:18; 11:1–4; John 8:1–11; Romans 3:25; Ephesians 5:2; James 5:16; 1 Peter 2:24; 1 John 1:9.

45: Forgiveness

In one of his prayer letters, Ed Silvoso says that, 'Ruth and I ministered to a group of approximately 150 Chinese ladies. Ruth spoke first, and then I began to share about intimacy in marriage from a biblical perspective. As I did so, all of a sudden I began to feel the pain that many of those ladies felt due to the abuse inflicted by the men in their lives. I was able literally to feel that pain. Nothing in that audience of Chinese ladies – who normally are neither expressive nor emotional – could have given me a clue as to what was going on inside their souls. I know it had to be God, and I had no choice but to respond.

'I told the ladies that I felt many of them had been abused – verbally, physically, and sexually, by men. I went on to give them specific examples. Some of them had been called 'idiot' or 'useless' by their fathers or brothers or husbands. Others had been taken advantage of sexually. As I did this, I could see tears rimming the eyes of many of them.

'At that point I told them, "I want to take the place of that man that has hurt you, who never asked your forgiveness, and I want to ask your forgiveness so that you can be healed". I had not inflicted those hurts, but the gender to which I belonged had. As a man, I was in a position to repent on behalf of my peers.

'I asked the ladies that wished to receive my plea and extend forgiveness stand up. Close to 60% of the audience did so. Many began to weep. Others cried out loud. A few were trembling. As I knelt down and asked for forgiveness, something came upon the group. It was a sublime moment. I believe that not only God, but angels were there ministering to those ladies.

'I told them, "Many of you are feeling pain, deep pain, pain that you have chosen to ignore because it has been so unbearable. Do not be afraid of it. The pain you are feeling now is pain on the way out, not on the way in. Let it come up so that Jesus can take it . . . " When I said this, the dam holding all that misery broke and this assembly of supposedly unemotional Chinese ladies simply broke before the Lord.

'There I was on my knees, like Nehemiah, asking for forgiveness for the sins of my ancestors and the sins of my own generation. Like the early Christians in Acts 2:43 I was enveloped by a divine sense of awe. I no longer had a message. I no longer was the feature speaker. God had manifested himself in our midst and his people were being set free. I literally watched inner healing take place. That evening, testimonies would be heard from every corner of the assembly of how God had set his people free.

'Finally, I stood up. As I wiped the tears from my eyes and I embraced Ruth, a song of joy flooded my soul and burst through my lips.'

Themes: Abuse, Family, Freedom, Grief, Healing – inner, Inner healing, Intimacy, Joy, Marriage, Men, Shame.

Scriptures: Exodus 34:6; Psalm 103:12; Nehemiah 9:17; Isaiah 38:17; 43:25; 61:1; Jeremiah 31:34; Daniel 9:1–27; Micah 7:19; Mark 2:10–12; Luke 4:18; Acts 2:42; 1 John 1:9.

46: Forgiveness

An elderly lady came into contact with Christians. She was a bitter person. Over a number of weeks she heard the Good News, but no one had told her to take the action which turned out to change her life.

On the top of her wardrobe was a small portable typewriter which she had not thought about for a long time. But now, each time she went in the room she could not get it out of her mind. Then she had the strange urge to write a letter to her sister whom she had not contacted for years and ask her forgiveness for a rift between them. Eventually she got the machine down and typed a letter.

Even before she posted it; as she was folding up the letter she said her body felt as if it was being washed all over and she had a sense of being forgiven.

The two sisters have been restored to each other.

Themes: Bitterness, Good Works, Healing – inner, Inner healing, Lord's Prayer, Parable – Unforgiving Servant, Reconciliation.

Scriptures: Psalms 32; 51; Matthew 18:21–35; Mark 11:25; Luke 11:1–4; Romans 12:14; 1 Corinthians 11:29–32; 1 Thessalonians 5:13.

47: Freedom

The story is told of an Arab called Bark who was kidnapped into slavery. He learned to tremble at a handclap and to come lumbering on command. One day a kind friend purchased his freedom. The friend provided him with money, and sent him on his way.

At first Bark tried to act out all the dreams of freedom he had harboured and dreamed of as a slave. He went to a restaurant and paid a waiter to wait on him. He bought a woman and bid her please him. But his dreams were soon used up, and freedom became a fearful burden. Then he met a tearful child. With the child he searched the city to secure some consoling toy. This was it. For the rest of his life Bark gave his freedom as a willing slave to the ragtaggle kids of the street.

Themes: Atonement, Cross, Good works, Materialism, Money, Redeemed, Rescued, Slavery.

Scriptures: Exodus 6:6; Psalm 77:14–15; Mark 10:45; Luke 24:21; John 1:29; 8:31–36; 1 Corinthians 1:30; 5:7; 6:19–20; 7:22–23; Galatians 3:13; 4:4–5; 5:1; Ephesians 1:7; 2:10; 5:2; 1 Timothy 2:6; Titus 2:14; Hebrews 9:15; 1 Peter 1:18–19; 1 John 2:2.

48: Freedom

The South American country, Bolivia is named after Simon Bolivar. Bolivar was born into a wealthy slave-owning family of nobles from Caracus in Venezuela. When he was studying in Madrid he was impressed by the closing scenes of the French Revolution. When he returned to South America he set about liberating the slaves. He led campaigns against the Spanish and became the president of what is now Colombia. The country Bolivia was named after him for he bought and freed all the slaves in that area.

Themes: Atonement, Cross, Freedom, Jesus – his work, Redeemed, Rescue.

Scriptures: Exodus 6:6; Psalm 77:14–15; Mark 10:45; Luke 24:21; John 1:29; 8:31–36; 1 Corinthians 1:30; 5:7; 6:19–20; 7:22–23; Galatians 3:13; 4:4–5; 5:1; Ephesians 1:7; 5:2; Titus 2:14; Hebrews 9:15; 1 Peter 1:18–19; 1 John 2:2.

49: Giving

In the book *The Church in the Market Place*, George Carey tells of a church rebuilding programme. In relation to the principle of going beyond our means he tells the story of a thirteen-year-old boy who had about £500 in his savings, and after talking with his parents came to see him because he wanted to loan it to the church free of interest, and for as long as they liked! It was times like these that showed him that sacrificial giving was running very deep in the congregation. People were diverting money into the building project from savings, holidays, life insurances and so on. George Carey said, 'All this indicated that our giving had passed from generosity to surrender of our possessions.'

Themes: Generosity, Giving, God – his provision, Materialism, Money, Offerings, Sacrificial giving, Tithing, Wealth.

Scriptures: Psalm 112:9; Isaiah 55:10–11; Mark 10:17–31; 12:41–44; Luke 19:1–10; 2 Corinthians 8; 9; 1 Timothy 6:17–19; Hebrews 13:5.

50: God – his care

Hudson Taylor was a missionary statesman in China in the last century. Part of the entry from his journal dated 18 November 1857 reads as follows. 'On Saturday, the 4th ... we supplied, as usual, a breakfast to the destitute poor, who came to the number of seventy . . . On that Saturday we paid all expenses, and provided for the morrow, after which we had not a single dollar left between us. How the Lord was going to provide for Monday we knew not . . . ' But he goes on to say, 'That very day the mail came in, a week sooner than was expected, and Mr. Jones received a bill for two hundred and fourteen dollars. We thanked God and took courage.' A note in the journal says, 'On Monday the poor had their breakfast as usual.'

Themes: Generosity, Giving, God – his provision, Missionaries, Poverty, Worry.

Scriptures: Genesis 15:1; 50:20; 1 Kings 17; Job 38:41; Psalms 37:5, 23–24; 55:22; 56:4–5; 91; 118:6; Proverbs 3:5–6; Isaiah 49:15; Malachi 3:8–10; Luke 12:4–7, 22–24; Romans 8:28; 2 Corinthians 8; 9; Hebrews 13:5; 1 Peter 5:7.

51: God – discovering

Young Irina lived in Odessa, on the north coast of the Black Sea during the Khrushchev years. She often wondered why the teachers bothered with the truckloads of words against God. She used to think, '(God) must exist – and he must be very powerful for them to fear him so greatly.'

It didn't often snow in Odessa. But, this particular day it was. Irina was looking out the window, ignoring what the teacher was saying. But, she said to herself, 'Okay, God . . . If you're so powerful, make it keep snowing.' That was Irina's first prayer. It was the largest snowfall for sixty years. Irina began to think about the God who teachers denied. She began to talk to him secretly, late at night. She had no idea what God wanted from her. Yet, the moment she thought this, an answer seemed to echo from within. 'Don't worry, you will find out what you need to know when the time comes.' She began to devour the great Russian books on her parents' shelves: Dostoevsky, Pushkin, Turgenev and Tolstoy. In these she found a reflection of the God whom she sensed was kind and all powerful. Then came the confusion of adolescence. Suddenly, her parents' beloved books offered no help. She realized she knew so little about Christ. All she had were a few quotes picked from various books. Irina began to write poetry to express her struggle to find God. One night, as she penned some lines, she felt a benevolent eye looking over her shoulder. She said, 'I shivered despite the delicious warmth, for I knew whose glance it was. He had not abandoned me. He was with me . . . and he didn't mind that I couldn't pray properly.'

Themes: Atheism, God – his existence, God – his nature, God – search for, God – with us, Prayer – answered, Prayer – difficulties, Prayer – first.

Scriptures: Psalms 37:3-5, 53:1; 145:10-13; Isaiah 7:14; 40:12-26; Jeremiah 10:1–16; Matthew 1:23; Luke 11:1–13; John 4:24; Acts 17:23–30; Romans 1:18–20; 8:26; Ephesians 6:18; Hebrew 10:6.

52: God – his presence

For twenty years Dr Helen Rosevere was a medical missionary in the Congo. In 1964, when the Simba rebellion occurred, she was attacked and captured by rebel forces. She was beaten and raped repeatedly. A few years later she had this to say in an interview:

> The rebels had decided to execute several of us. Only too quickly the moment came when we were actually standing in front of the firing line. If someone had asked me earlier if I could have been a martyr, I would have answered definitely 'No, I'm not built that way.' But as we faced those guns, certain to be killed at any second, we were actually singing the praises of God. We suddenly experienced God's presence and joyfully anticipated our reunion with him in heaven. God simply swept our fears away. Miraculously, at the last moment the rebels decided not to execute us. In fact, I can remember one other late night experience where this overwhelming consciousness of God's presence came to me, that he was there, that he was in charge and that he knew what was happening. It was as almost as if he said to me, 'They are not beating you or raping you; these are not your sufferings; these are my sufferings. All I'm asking is the loan of your body.'

Themes: Fellowship of Suffering, Martyrdom, Missionaries, Persecution, Praise, Rejection, Suffering.

Scriptures: Psalm 34:1; Matthew 28:20; John 15:18–19; 16:32–33; 17:14; Acts 18:10; Ephesians 5:20; Hebrews 13:15; 1 Peter 4:13; 1 John 3:13.

53: God – his sovereignty

Some years ago, Ray Steadman and his wife were part way through a long car trip. In the motel the night before, Susan, their little daughter had developed a fever. But it didn't seem serious. As they drove along, suddenly, Susan went into convulsions. Her eyes turned up, her body began to jerk. She was obviously in considerable danger. Ray's heart seemed to miss a beat. He stopped the car there and then. He grabbed Susan, and stumbled across the road to a farmhouse that happened to be visible nearby. It was just beginning to get light when he frantically kicked on the door as he held Susan. A cautious woman opened the door a little. 'My daughter is very sick. She's having convulsions. Do you have a bath where we can put her in cool water?' The lady was so taken aback she did not really speak. She just opened the door a little more and mumbled and pointed. Ray pushed the door right open, strode down the passage to the back of the house and ran a bath to cool off his treasured girl. Then he rang a local doctor to make an appointment.

The incredible thing is that there was not another house for many miles around. And, of all the homes in the area, Ray and his wife found out that this was the only one with a bath and a telephone.

Themes: Coincidence, Fear, God – his care, God – his provision, Healing, Miracles, Worry.

Scriptures: Genesis 15:1; 50:19–20; 1 Kings 17; Job 38:41; Psalms 27:1; 37:5; 23–24; 55:22; 56:4–5; 91; 118:6; Proverbs 3:5–6; Isaiah 49:15; Luke 12:4–7, 22–34; Romans 8:28; 1 Peter 5:7.

54: Greed

There is an old legend about a greedy man and an envious man who were walking along when they were overtaken by a stranger who got to know them. After a while he said, as he departed from them, that he would give each of them a gift. Whoever made a wish first would get what he wanted and the other would get a double portion of what the first had asked for. The greedy man knew what he wanted but he was afraid to make his wish because he wanted the double portion for himself and did not want the other to get it. And the envious man felt the same way, and he was also unwilling to wish first. After a while the envious man grabbed the greedy man by the throat and said he would choke him to death unless he made his wish. And at that the greedy man replied, 'Very well. I will make my wish – I wish to made blind in one eye.' Immediately he lost the sight of one eye and his envious companion went blind in both.

Themes: Envy, Fruit of the Spirit, Works of the flesh.

Scriptures: Mark 15:10; Romans 12; Galatians 5:16–26.

55: Greed

In the movie *Wall Street*, Gordon Gekko is played by Michael Douglas. He is a cunning unprincipled multi-millionnaire corporate raider. One day he speaks to a meeting of spellbound shareholders who are worried about a takeover bid. He declares,

> '... ladies and gentlemen, greed – for lack of a better word – is good. Greed is right. Greed works. Greed clarifies, cuts through and captures the essence of the evolutionary spirit. Greed, in all of its forms – greed for life, for money, for love, for knowledge – has marked the upward surge of mankind ...'

Later in the film, Gordon's friend Bud asks, 'Tell me, Gordon, when does it all end? ... How many yachts can you water-ski behind? How much is enough?'

Themes: Generosity, Giving, God – his provision, Materialism, Money, Offerings, Sacrificial giving, Tithing, Wealth.

Scriptures: Psalm 112:9; Isaiah 55:10–11; Matthew 6:19–21; Mark 10:17–31; 12:41–44; Luke 19:1–10; 2 Corinthians 8; 9; 1 Timothy 6:17–19; Hebrews 13:5.

56: Grief

In the very early hours of Sunday morning, 6 January 1985, a couple learned the shocking news that their younger son of eighteen had put a gun under his chin and shot himself. When the minister went to the house there was a profound sadness over the people gathered there. In some of the rooms, and outside as well, there were friends and members of the extended family sitting or standing in disbelief. Some were openly and uncontrollably crying. The only place the minister could to talk with the parents was in their bedroom. They embraced each other and shared the grief as much as they could. Then they sat on the bed. The minister prayed for them. Then he invited them to ask God to take control of their lives in the midst of tragedy and fill them with his Spirit.

Here is how the father related the event exactly six months later. 'I . . . asked God to refill my life with the Holy Spirit and almost instantly I felt a warm peaceful feeling throughout my whole body. It was like being defrosted, only from the inside out. Since that time I have been at peace with God and the world . . . Don't get me wrong, Christians do cry, and I still cry for my family and my son, but I am peaceful when I do.'

Themes: Comfort, Death, God – his peace, Holy Spirit – filling, Peace, Suicide.

Scriptures: 2 Samuel 12; Psalms 6:5–7; 23:4; 46; 55:22; 119:28; Isaiah 25:8; 53:3–4; Hosea 13:14; Matthew 5:4; John 11; Romans 5:1–5; 1 Corinthians 15:54–56; 2 Corinthians 1:3–7; 1 Thessalonians 4:13–18; James 1:2–4; 1 Peter 5:6–7.

57: *Grief*

After the death of his wife, a Christian publisher in Britain wrote:

> How does one pray when the eyes are filled with tears? In those dark days of loss, anxiety, self-pity, and unanswered questions, I made a discovery. *I didn't have to pray*. No preacher, no book, had ever told me that. God's love, his understanding, his companionship, were not dependent on my prayers. In these special circumstances I didn't have to seek him – he was there. 'Talk to me again, when you're ready,' he seemed to say. 'I'll be waiting and listening.'

Themes: Comfort, Death, God – his grace, God – his love, God – his peace, God – his presence, God – his understanding, Prayer – difficulties.

Scriptures: 2 Samuel 12; Psalms 6:5–7; 23:4; 46; 55:22; 119:28; Isaiah 25:8; 53:3–4; Hosea 13:14; Matthew 5:4; John 11; Romans 5:1–5; 8:26–28; 1 Corinthians 15:54–56; 2 Corinthians 1:3–7; Ephesians 2:8–9; 1 Thessalonians 4:13–18; James 1:2–4; 1 Peter 5:6–7.

58: *Guidance*

Two men were walking down a noisy and busy street. One of them was a scientist; an entomologist – a bug catcher. Suddenly he stopped and asked his friend, 'Can you hear that?'

'All I can hear is the noise of passing people and the roar of traffic,' said the friend.

'Yes, and I can also hear a cricket,' put in the scientist.

Going over to the wall of a tall office block he moved a small loose stone in the footpath. Under it was the cricket which had been making its shrill music. As they continued along the friend asked how on earth he could hear the cricket above all the noise. To show how easy it was the scientist took out a twenty cent piece and dropped it on the ground in the middle of the rushing crowd. You can guess what happened. A number of people instantly stopped and looked around for the coin which made the barely audible yet recognizable tinkling sound of a coin.

Themes: Listening to God, Money, Obedience, Prayer.

Scriptures: Exodus 13:21–22; 33:14; Deuteronomy 4:30; 31:6, 8; 1 Kings 19:11–12; Psalms 23:4; 25:1–4, 9; 32:8; 48:14; 66:12; 138:7; Proverbs 3:5–6; Isaiah 43:2; Daniel 3:25, 28; John 10:27; 16:13.

59: *Guidance*

On the morning of 14 January 1909, a Chilean night watchman in Valparaiso fell asleep. Suddenly Jesus Christ appeared to him in a dream. The man had been a Christian and member of the local Methodist church for some time, but this had never happened to him before.

Jesus looked at him and said in a gentle but firm voice, 'Wake up. I want to speak to you.'

'Yes, Lord!' the startled man replied.

'Go to your pastor and tell him to gather some of the most spiritual people of the congregation. They are to pray together every day. I intend to baptize them with tongues of fire.'

Sleep was gone. The man hurried to find Willis Hoover, his pastor, and tell him about the dream. Hoover, in fact, had already been praying and was expecting something like this. The next afternoon at five o'clock a group began to meet. By April the revival had come. In July there were 363 in the Sunday School. In September there were 527. Each Sunday there were 800 to 900 in church.

Themes: Dreams, Listening to God, Obedience Revival, Visions.

Scriptures: Exodus 13:21–22; 33:14; Deuteronomy 4:30; 31:6, 8; 1 Kings 19:11–12; Psalms 23:4; 25:1–4, 9; 32:8; 48:14; 66:12; 138:7; Proverbs 3:5–6; Isaiah 43:2; Daniel 3:25, 28; Joel 2:28; John 10:27; 16:13; Acts 2:17; 10:9–16.

60: *Guidance*

Smith was in deep trouble. He was sitting on his roof during a terrible flood, and the water was already up to his feet. He was a Christian and began to pray that the Lord would provide a miracle and rescue him.

Before long, a fellow in a boat paddled by and shouted, 'Can I give you a lift to higher ground?'

'No, thanks,' said Smith. 'I have faith in the Lord and he will save me.'

Soon the water rose to Smith's waist. At this point, a motorboat pulled up and someone called out,

'Can I give you a lift to higher ground?'

'No, thanks. I have faith in the Lord and he will save me.'

Later a helicopter flew by, and Smith was now standing on the roof with water up to his neck.

'Grab the rope,' yelled the pilot 'I'll pull you up'.

'No, thanks,' said Smith. 'I have faith in the Lord and he will save me'.

But then after hours of treading water, poor, exhausted Smith drowned and went to his reward.

As he arrived at the Pearly Gates, Smith met his Maker and complained about this turn of events.

'Tell me, Lord,' he said, 'I had such faith in you to save me and you let me down. What happened?'

The Lord replied, 'What do you want from me? I sent you two boats and a helicopter!'

Themes: Faith, Humour, Listening to God, Obedience.

Scriptures: Exodus 13:21–22; 33:14; Deuteronomy 4:30; 31:6, 8; 1 Kings 19:11–12; Psalms 23:4; 25:1–4, 9; 32:8; 48:14; 66:12; 138:7; Proverbs 3:5–6; Isaiah 43:2; Daniel 3:25, 28; Joel 2:28; John 10:27; 16:13; Acts 2:17; 10:9–16.

61: Guilt

Velma Barfield was convicted of murder and in 1986 was executed by lethal injection. Shortly before she died she wrote:

> I ... want to make it clear that I am not blaming ... drugs for my crimes. I am not blaming my troubled childhood or the marriage problems ... I bear the responsibility for the wrongs I have done. I know those things influenced me, but they are my sins and my crimes.

Themes: Capital Punishment, Confession, Drugs, Marriage difficulties, Murder, Parenting, Repentance, Sin.

Scriptures: Exodus 20:13; Leviticus 5:5; 26:40–42; Deuteronomy 5:17; Psalms 31:10; 32:5; 51; Proverbs 20:9; Matthew 18:21–35; Mark 11:25; John 8:34–36; Acts 2:38; James 5:16; 1 John 1:8–9.

62: Healing

A dad could hear his wife in the next room trying to comfort their daughter, who was in the throes of a week-long illness. As a man who claimed that God answered prayer for healing he felt he should go in and pray for his daughter. But he had prayed for his children so many times before when they were sick, and never did it seem to make much difference.

'How can I have faith when nothing ever happens?' he said to himself. 'Where do you get faith?'

The dad then recalled the passage in Romans 10:17 where Paul talks about faith coming from hearing about Christ. So he picked up his Bible and went into his wife and his little girl. Sitting on the edge of the bed, he started to read aloud the stories of Jesus healing the sick. Something began to happen inside dad. He grew more and more confident that Jesus *was* able to heal his daughter. He could see the same trust growing in his daughter's eyes. Then, together, they asked Jesus to make her well. From that moment she recovered rapidly.

Themes: Faith, Healing, Illness, Miracles, Prayer, Prayer – unanswered, Sickness, Signs and wonders.

Scriptures: Matthew 8:5–13; 9:27–31; Mark 1:29–31, 40–44; 2:1–12; 3:1–6; 5:24–34; 7:31–37; 8:22–26; 10:46–52; Luke 13:10–17; 14:1–6; John 4:46–54; 9:1–34; 11:25–26; Acts 2:22; 5:12; 14:8–18; Romans 5:18–19; 10:17; 1 Corinthians 12:9, 28, 30; Galatians 3:2, 5; 1 Thessalonians 1:5; James 5:14–15; 1 Peter 1:13.

63: Healing

Pamela Reddy had been told by doctors that she needed her diseased right kidney removed. She was also recovering from hepatitis. She had been exposed to tuberculosis at the hospital where she worked. And due to injury to her shoulder and neck her left arm did not function well or without pain (she is left-handed). Doctors told her she would never have full use of her arm or freedom from pain. One Sunday she came for special prayer at her church. A married couple, George and Pam, laid hands on her and prayed. The pain in Pamela's kidney disappeared, and her shoulder gained mobility. Over the next few weeks other prayers were answered. Eventually, she underwent a physical examination for her new job. All the tests came back negative. There was no kidney disease and no residue of hepatitis or TB. Her neck has straightened, the bones in her shoulder are no longer rubbing and she has the full range of movement in her arm with no pain.

Themes: Laying on of hands, Miracles, Prayer, Signs and wonders.

Scriptures: Matthew 8:5–13; 9:27–31; Mark 1:29–31, 40–44; 2:1–12; 3:1–6; 5:24–34; 7:31–37; 8:22–26; 10:46–52; Luke 13:10–17; 14:1–6; John 4:46–54; 9:1–34; 11:25–26; Acts 2:22; 5:12; 14:8–18; Romans 15:18–19; 1 Corinthians 12:9, 28, 30; 2 Corinthians 12:12; Galatians 3:5; 1 Thessalonians 1:5; James 5:14–15; 1 Peter 1:13.

64: Healing

John White and his wife were in Malaysia and praying for a two-year-old child. Her body was completely covered with raw, weeping eczema sores. She ran around the room restlessly so that her parents had to catch her to bring her struggling to John and his wife.

They began to pray and extended their hands to lay them on her. The instant their hands touched her she fell into profound and relaxed slumber in her mum's arms. John said, 'I shall never forget our sense of exhilaration and excitement as the weeping areas began to dry up, their borders shrinking visibly before our eyes like the shores of lakes in time of drought.'

Themes: Joy, Laying on of hands, Miracles, Prayer, Signs and wonders.

Scriptures: Matthew 8:5–13; 9:27–31; Mark 1:29–31, 40–44; 2:1–12; 3:1–6; 5:24–34; 7:31–37; 8:22–26; 10:46–52; Luke 13:10–17; 14:1–6; John 4:46–54; 9:1–34; 11:25–26; Acts 2:22; 5:12; 8:8; 14:8–18; Romans 15:18–19; 1 Corinthians 12:9, 28, 30; 2 Corinthians 12:12; Galatians 3:5; 1 Thessalonians 1:5; James 5:14–15; 1 Peter 1:13.

65: Healing

Colin and Caroline Urquhart were staying with Charles and Joyce and their family, while Colin was ministering for a few days in Cornwall. Colin and his wife were sitting having a leisurely cup of coffee in someone's home when they heard screams.

One of the boys came rushing into the kitchen: 'Dad, there's been an accident'. Charles didn't wait to hear any more. He ran out of the house and across the yard, closely followed by Joyce.

On the previous evening he had been speaking about the prayer promises of Jesus and what it means to pray with faith or trust, knowing that God is going to answer you. Colin and his wife were praying when Charles carried ten-year-old Joanna into the room.

In the garage the children had been melting down lead to pour into moulds, to make gifts for Christmas. One of them dropped a cold piece of metal into the container causing some of the molten mixture to fly into Joanne's face. Some of the lead had gone into both eyes. Can you imagine the effect of molten lead on eyes?

It took her mother nearly forty minutes to remove all the pieces of metal. During that time they all prayed, silently and aloud, with Joanna and for her. But all the time they thanked the Lord that there would be no damage to the eyes, and praised him for his healing.

Joanna was obviously in considerable distress, so once the metal had been removed from her eyes, they asked the Lord to give her a good sleep, so that she would not suffer from shock after such an experience.

She slept, and at 5pm was downstairs having a meal. Joanna's eyes were not even bloodshot! And it was subsequently confirmed that she had suffered no damage to them at all.

Themes: Faith, Miracles, Prayer, Signs and wonders.

Scriptures: Matthew 8:5–13; 9:27–31; Mark 1:29–31; 40–44; 2:1–12; 3:1–6; 5:24–34; 7:31–37; 8:22–26; 10:46–52; Luke 13:10–17; 14:1–6; John 4:46–54; 9:1–34; 11:25–26; Acts 2:22; 5:12; 8:8; 14:8–18; Romans 15:18–19; 1 Corinthians 12:9, 28, 30; 2 Corinthians 12:12; Galatians 3:5; 1 Thessalonians 1:5; James 5:14–15; 1 Peter 1:13.

66: Heaven

A little boy was caught up to no good. He was asked rather harshly by his mother, 'How do you expect to get in to heaven?' He thought for a moment and then said, 'Well I'll just run in and out and keep slamming the door till they say, "For goodness sake come in or stay out." Then I'll go in'.

Themes: Discipline, Eschatology, Hell, Hope, Life after death, Parable – Great Banquet, Parenting.

Scriptures: Luke 14:15–24; John 10:9; 11:25–26; 14:1–6; Romans 5:2; 8:18, 29; 1 Corinthians 13:12; 15; Ephesians 1:11–12; 2:18; 3:12; 6:1–4; Colossians 1:12; 3:20–21; Hebrews 3:6; 1 John 3:2.

67: Help

Paul Fifield is nineteen and comes from Girton in Cambridgeshire. He wanted to become a drama student. Hoping to promote his career as an actor he modelled as a male nude to be made from plaster. Unfortunately Kate Freeland, the art student making the piece of art, used wall plaster instead of plaster of Paris for the full-body mould. Paul was in agony when she tried to break off the solid cast. He said, 'I was as stiff as a plank'.

Relief came when firemen took Paul to Addenbrookes Hospital. There, staff gave him an anesthetic while they hammered off the plaster to reveal only Y-fronts and socks on Paul's naked body. He said, 'Kate had a book on how to do it, but I don't think she got further than the preface'.

Themes: Freedom, Humour, New life, New nature, Old life, Old nature, Trust.

Scriptures: Mark 10:52; Romans 6:6; 13:14; 2 Corinthians 5:7; Galatians 3:27; Ephesians 2:1–10; 4:22–24; Colossians 3:8–14; 1 Peter 2:1; Revelation 21:4–5.

68: Holiness

When Stanley was with Livingstone in Africa he saw the great man slumped over his bed one night. Stanley rushed in and asked Livingstone if he was all right.

'Yes, I'm just reading my Bible through one more time to see if I have to adjust anything in my life before I meet Jesus'.

Themes: Bible reading, Christian living, Saints, Sanctification.

Scriptures: Leviticus 19:2; Isaiah 29:13; Joel 2:12–13; Matthew 15:19–20; Romans 6:11, 19; 2 Corinthians 7:1; Galatians 2:20; Ephesians 2:10; 5:3–5; 1 Thessalonians 4:1–8; 1 Timothy 2:15; 2 Timothy 2:21; 3:16–17; Titus 2:14; 3:1; Hebrews 12:14; 1 Peter 1:15–16; 2:12, 15; 3 John 11.

69: Hospitality

It was a particular Friday afternoon, in downtown Chicago. There was a poorly dressed man with two dollars in his pocket. A wino? No, the man was a minister from Mississippi. As a way of identifying with human need, he and a number of others had been dropped off in various localities to fend for themselves as best they could for the whole weekend.

After wandering around on the Sunday, he came to a large downtown church holding an evening service. After the service was over, he stood on the front steps and waited. No one spoke. Then he went across the street where a group of *real* winos was passing around a bottle. Immediately they called him 'brother', offered him a drink, and asked if he had a 'pad' for the night. One even tried to give him his last thirty-seven cents.

Themes: Entertaining, Love of neighbour, Parable – Good Samaritan, Rejection.

Scriptures: Genesis 18:1–8; 19:1; Exodus 22:21; Leviticus 19:10; Numbers 35:9–35; Deuteronomy 10:19; 23:3–4; Joshua 20:1–9; Judges 6:17–23; 8:5–17; 13:15–21; 19:15; 1 Samuel 25:2–38; 2 Kings 4:8–10; Job 31:32; Isaiah 58:7; Zephaniah 1:7; Mark 2:15–17; Luke 7:36–50; 10:29–37, 38–42; Romans 12:13–14; Galatians 6:10; Colossians 4:10; 1 Timothy 3:2; 5:10; Titus 1:8; Hebrews 13:2; 1 Peter 4:9.

70: Humility

The eyes of the world have often been on Linford Christie. He is Britain's greatest sprinter. He has won more than twenty medals including an Olympic gold at Barcelona in 1992. Linford is also one of Britain's richest sportsmen with appearance money of about thirty thousand pounds a race and sponsorship deals. He shops in Paris and New York.

Christie owes much of his success to an unlikely hero, sixty-three-year-old Ron Roddan who has been his coach for sixteen years. Ron is a former geologist who is rarely seen in public. Ron refuses to be paid for his coaching, choosing to live on his pension after being made redundant some years ago. 'I don't coach people for money but because I enjoy the sport,' says Ron. Rather then accompany Linford to track meetings, Ron prefers to analyse Linford's races on television. 'You have to respect Ron's wish to be in the background,' says Linford. 'He lets my feet do the talking.' John Regis, another sprinter says, 'Linford gets all the acclaim but without Ron he would never have had much success.'

Themes: Apprenticing, Encouragement, Fame, Greatness, Jesus – character, John the Baptist, Moses, Leadership, Mentoring, Money, Parable – Pharisee and the Tax Collector, Purpose, Retirement, Service, Sport, Success, Support, Teaching.

Scriptures: Numbers 12:3; Deuteronomy 18:2; 2 Samuel 22:36; Psalms 18:35, 113:5–6; Proverbs 3:34; 15:33; 18:12; 25:6–7; Daniel 5:22–31; Matthew 11:29; Mark 1:7; 9:33–37; Luke 1:16, 52; 8:9–14; 9:46–48; 11:43; 14:7–14; 18:9–14; 20:46; John 1:6–9; Romans 12:3; 1 Corinthians 2:16; 10:13; Ephesians 4:2; Philippians 2:1–11; Colossians 3:12; James 2:2–4; 4:10; 1 Peter 5:5–6.

71: Incarnation

One day man came to God on his heavenly throne and said to him, 'Which do you think is harder, to be man or to be God?'

'Being God is much harder,' God answered. 'I have a whole universe to worry about, planets and galaxies. All you have to worry about is your family and your job'.

'True enough,' said man. 'But you have infinite time and infinite power. The hard part in being a man is not doing the job, but doing it within the limits of human strength and the human life span.'

God answered, 'You don't know what you're talking about. It's much harder to be God.'

Man replied, 'I don't know how you can say that so confidently when you've never been human and I've never been God. What do you say we change places for just one second, so you can know the feeling of being man and I can know what it feels like to be God. Just for one second, that's all, and then we'll change back.'

God didn't want to, but man kept begging and pleading, and finally relented. They changed places. Man became God and God became human.

And the story goes on to say that, once man sat on the divine throne, he refused to give God back his place, and ever since then man has ruled the world and God has been in exile.

Themes: Alienation, Fall, Parable – Prodigal Son, Pride, Rebellion.

Scriptures: Genesis 3; Job 38:1–40:2; 40:6–41:34; Luke 15:8–10; Romans 1:18–32; Ephesians 2:1–12; 4:18.

72: Incarnation

In March 1993 the Serbian attack on Bosnia besieged the town of Srebrenica. There were mortar attacks on civilians causing terrible suffering.

General Philippe Morillon was the commander of the United Nation forces. He decided to shield the citizens from attack by making Srebrenica his centre of operations. He refused an offer from the Serbs of safe passage out of the town. The citizens of Srebrenica described the General as 'the only way of salvation'.

Morillon stayed there for eight days to show his solidarity with the people, and to act as a human shield. Then he left. On 19 March, 1993 he led a convoy back into the besieged city. He brought supplies and took out the sick and wounded.

Themes: Adam and Christ, Exodus, God – his love, Jesus – his work, Leadership, Protection, Rescue, Victory.

Scriptures: Luke 4:18; John 1:14; 14:6; Acts 26:18; Romans 5:12–21; Galatians 1:4; 2:20; Colossians 1:13; 2:15.

73: Incarnation

One night in 1963, a theatre production was part way through its performance in the old Birmingham Repertory Theatre, Station Street. One of the actors walked across the stage. He was holding a transistor radio on his shoulder. It was tuned to the local station, playing pop music. It was all part of the play. Then, suddenly, as the actors spoke their lines the music was interrupted. A news flash announced, 'President Kennedy has been assassinated'. To save interrupting the play the actor quickly snapped off the radio. But it was too late. The audience had heard the news. As much as they tried, the news meant the actors could not carry on as before.

Themes: Change, God – voice of, Murder.

Scriptures: Genesis 18:1–15; Exodus 3:1–6; 1 Samuel 3:1–4:1; Isaiah 7:14; Matthew 1:23; John 1:1–18.

74: Incarnation

A salesman had been away from home for several days at a regional conference. The closing session had overrun its time and, as soon as it was over, he hurried with his friends to the mainline station. They had barely enough time to catch a train which would get them back early enough to spend some of the evening with their families. If they missed that particular train, there would be a considerable wait before the next, and they would be very late home.

As the group charged through the terminal, the man inadvertently kicked over a small table supporting a vendor's box of fruit. Apples tumbled out and rolled across the floor in all directions, but the men rushed on to the platform with only seconds to spare before the train left. As they boarded the train, the man responsible for the accident stopped in his tracks, almost unable to move. His colleagues urged him to catch the train but, deep inside, he felt desperately unhappy. Should he go on or go back? He noticed a young boy, about ten years old, standing by the table, selling the apples.

More than anything, he longed to be back with his family. However, waving goodbye to his puzzled friends, he briskly made his way back to the main concourse. People were rushing for their trains, dodging the apples. Many had been kicked here and there by hurrying travellers and the man was puzzled that the lad had done nothing whatever to retrieve his apples. As he got closer, he realized why the boy was just standing there, dazed and helpless. He was blind.

Quickly the salesman began to collect the apples. Setting up the table again, he could see that many of them were badly bruised. Opening his wallet, he took out a note, pressed it into the boy's hand, saying, 'Here, please take this five pounds for the damage we did. Hope we haven't spoilt your day.' Slowly he began to walk away when, above the noise of the station, he heard the loud voice of the boy calling after him 'Sir, are you Jesus?'

Themes: Body of Christ, Fruit of the Spirit, Good works, Humility, Imitation of Christ, Kindness, Servant Evangelism, Service.

Scriptures: Exodus 22:1–3; Numbers 12:3; Psalm 113:5–6; Proverbs 15:33; 18:12; Matthew 5:16; Romans 12:5; 1 Corinthians 4:16; 6:20; 11:1; 12:27; Galatians 5:22; Ephesians 2:10; Philippians 2:5; 3:17; 1 Thessalonians 1:6; 2:14;

2 Thessalonians 3:7–9; 2 Timothy 3:17; Hebrews 12:1–3;
1 Peter 2:12, 21; 1 John 2:6; 3:17; 4:7–11.

75: *Injustice*

For Robert Hearsch, his job became a nightmare that wouldn't end. For four years Hearsch had been a successful supervisor for Hughes Aircraft. Then General Motors took over the company – and his career took a nose dive. As part of the restructuring, he was put in charge of buying pens and pencils. He found orders backlogged and records in disarray. He spent most of his days appeasing angry secretaries. However, he stayed on, arriving early, leaving late, working through his breaks. But, as Hearsch tells the story, things only got worse. His supervisors hinted that his position might be phased out. They ignored his diligence and recorded small mistakes into his file. They even left him off the guest list for the department office party. The pressure took its toll. Hearsch lost twenty pounds. His marriage ended. He suffered a minor nervous breakdown. Hearsch finally filed a workers' compensation claim, blaming his health and emotional problems on Hughes. He subsequently accepted a $20,000 settlement from the company, which refuses to comment on the case. The money he says, is small consolation. 'I lost my wife, my house and my career'.

Themes: Anxiety, Family, Pressure, Stress, Suffering, Unemployment, Work, Worry.

Scriptures: Psalms 34:4; 46; 55:22; Matthew 6:19–34; 10:28; Luke 12:5, 22–31; Romans 12:12; Philippians 4:6; 2 Timothy 1:7; Hebrews 13:5–6; 1 Peter 5:5–6.

76: Integrity

Søren Kiekegaard told a parable about a man who was walking down a street in Europe many decades ago. He saw a sign in the window that said 'Pants Pressed'. He went into the store, slipped behind the counter, and started to take off his trousers. A clerk saw him and said, 'What are you doing?'

The man replied, 'I want to have my pants pressed. I saw your sign in the window.' To which the clerk replied, 'Oh, we don't press pants here. We just paint signs.'

Themes: Consistency, Humour, Parable.

Scriptures: Matthew 5:37; James 5:12.

77: Integrity

When Standard Oil was setting up its operations in Indonesia the executives were looking for a national director. They were told that the best qualified person was a full-time Christian worker. Standard Oil approached the man offering him a massive salary. He declined the offer. The executives raised the offer. Still the Christian worker declined. 'Well name your salary,' they ended up saying. But he replied, 'Oh, the salary is big enough, but the job isn't big enough!'

Themes: Call, Career, Leadership, Materialism, Mission, Money, Purpose, Sacrifice.

Scriptures: Exodus 18:21; Deuteronomy 1:13; Isaiah 6:1–13; Mark 3:13–19; 6:7–13; Luke 9:1–6; 10:1–20.

78: Jesus – character

Dostoevsky was a Russian novelist. When he arrived at a Siberian prison camp on Christmas Eve 1849, two women slipped him some money hidden in a copy of the New Testament. While the guard momentarily turned away, they suggested he should search the pages thoroughly.

Later he found a twenty-five rouble bank note. Although the money was useful it was the New Testament he treasured. He read it from cover to cover, pondering every word and learning much of it by heart. Here is his conclusion on Jesus.

> I believe that there is nothing lovelier, deeper, more sympathetic, more rational, more manly and more perfect than the Saviour. I say to myself with jealous love that not only is there no one else like him but there could be no one else.

Themes: Bible, Memorization, Persecution, Servant.

Scriptures: Isaiah 52:13–53:12; Matthew 11:29; Mark 10:45; Luke 10:29–37; John 1:1–18; 2 Corinthians 10:1; Philippians 2:1–11; Colossians 1:15–20; 2 Timothy 3:16; 1 Peter 1:18–19; John 1:1–5; 3:17.

79: Jesus – imitating

The Jews of a small Russian town were eagerly awaiting the arrival of a Rabbi. This was going to be a rare event so they spent a lot of time preparing the questions they were going to put to the holy man.

When he finally arrived and they met him in the Town Hall, he could sense the tension in the atmosphere as all prepared to listen to the answers he had for them.

He said nothing at first; he just gazed into their eyes, and hummed a haunting melody. Soon everyone began to hum. He started to sing and they sang along with him. He swayed and danced in solemn, measured steps. The audience followed suit. Soon they became so involved in the dance, so absorbed in its movements that they were lost to everything else on earth.

It was nearly an hour before the dance slowed down to a halt. With the tension drained out of their inner being everyone sat in the silent peace that pervaded the room. Then the Rabbi spoke the only words he pronounced that evening, 'I trust I have answered your questions'.

Themes: Dance, Discipleship, Peace, Unity.

Scriptures: 1 Corinthians 4:16; 11:1; Philippians 2:5; 3:17; 1 Thessalonians 1:6; 2:14; 2 Thessalonians 3:6, 9; Hebrews 12:1–3; 1 Peter 2:21; 1 John 2:6; 5:6–12.

80: Jesus – most important

The theologian Nels Ferre died a few years ago. Until the age of thirteen Nels lived with his poor family in Norway. They could not afford to educate their children. An aunt and uncle in the United States were childless. They wrote to Nels's parents and offered to raise him as their own and give him a good education. The parents accepted.

It was a wrenching experience for a boy of thirteen to be taken from his land and family, perhaps never to see them again, and to go to a new country with virtual strangers. Nels was close to his mother and he longed for a word from her that would sustain him. Through the day before he was to catch the ship his mother was silent. Through supper he yearned for a word . . . but there was silence.

After supper, the same. Nels went to bed and cried himself to sleep. The next morning at breakfast still no word. On the way to the village there was no sound from her. Finally as the train moved out of the station, Nels' last glimpse of his mother was one he never forgot: with tears streaming down her cheeks she held a scrawled note for him to read: 'Remember Jesus most of all'. His mother's last message pointed him to one who would be most important in moulding his life.

Themes: Following Jesus, Grief, Jesus – the head, Parenting, Separation, Worship.

Scriptures: John 1:1–18; 20:28; 1 Corinthians 4:16; 11:1; Ephesians 4:15; Philippians 2:5–11; 2:5; 3:17; Colossians 1:15–20; 2:19; 1 Thessalonians 1:6; 2:14; 2 Thessalonians 3:6, 9; Hebrews 1:1–14; 12:1–3; 1 Peter 2:21; 1 John 2:6; 5:6–12.

81: Judgement

A man was walking on the beach and found a magic lamp. When he rubbed it a genie appeared who told him he had one wish. Immediately the man asked for a copy of the stock market page from a newspaper printed one year later.

Suddenly the newspaper was in his hands. The genie had disappeared. With greed in his heart he scanned the columns, deciding what to invest in, knowing ahead of time what profitable stocks he could buy.

Turning the page, he noticed an obituary column. His name was at the top of the list.

Themes: Death, Envy, Fruit of the Spirit, Greed, Materialism, Wealth, Works of the flesh.

Scriptures; Psalms 34:1; 71:6; Hosea 14:2; Matthew 5:12; 6:19–21; Mark 15:10; Acts 11:22–26; 15:41; Romans 5:3–5; 12; 14:7–8, 19; 1 Corinthians 10:23; 2 Corinthians 5:15; 12:1–13; Galatians 2:20; 5:16–26; 6:9; Ephesians 4:29; 5:20; Philippians 1:21; 4:12; 1 Thessalonians 5:11; Hebrews 10:34; 13:15; James 1:2–4; 1 Peter 1:7; 2:5.

82: Leadership

Mike Delcavo is a cross-country runner. Recently he was running in the cross–country championship held in Riverside California. Only five of the 128 competitors completed the 10,000 metre course. At one point 123 runners missed a turn. Mike began waving for fellow runners to follow him. He was able to convince only four other runners to go with him. The press asked him what his competitors thought of his mid-race decision not to follow the crowd. Mike said they thought it was funny that he went the right way.

Themes: Courage, Distractions, False prophets, Following Jesus.

Scriptures: Deuteronomy 30:19–20; Jeremiah 21:8; Matthew 7:13–20; 24:11; Mark 13:21–23; Luke 13:24; John 10:7; 14:6; 1 Corinthians 7:35; 2 Corinthians 11:13–15; Galatians 6:9; 2 Peter 2:1; 1 John 4:1.

83: Leadership

A couple decided to hire a small plane. He had been a pilot for thirteen years. They set off for a small town 100 kilometres away to have a snack and then fly home. At one point in the flight home the husband remarked that he felt a little faint. And, in an instant, he collapsed in his seat. His face went completely white and his eyes rolled back in his head. The wife did not have the slightest idea how to fly the plane. She pressed the transmitter button on the microphone and cried out, 'Help me. Help me. I can't fly this aeroplane'. The radio was tuned to a frequency used by many pilots and air traffic controllers. Her frantic message was picked up by dozens of very helpful people. Suddenly there were voices saying, 'Follow a highway . . .' 'Fly towards the sun . . .' 'Turn on the landing light . . .'

Listening to this babble on the airwaves was a flight instructor. He ran to his plane, a small Cessna. He took off to try the impossible: find the voice in the sky asking for help. He waited for a lull in the transmission. Then he asked all the other transmitters to leave the frequency so he could make radio contact with the endangered lady. 'Madam, what is your name?' he asked. She stated her name. He calmly introduced himself and began to establish a rapport with her. All the time he was scanning the skies looking for the little plane. Then he saw a plane with its landing light on. 'Can you turn your landing light off?' The light went off. It was her. He flew his plane in front of her to show the woman he was there. Then he manoeuvred his plane just a little behind and to the side of her. He explained that he was an experienced flying instructor. Calmly and quietly he taught her the basics of flying. As they came to the airfield the instructor gave more detailed help. They flew over the strip first and then made the final approach. The woman was able to land the plane and walk away quite unhurt.

Themes: Apprenticing, Courage, Discipleship, Example, Faith, Following, Imitating Jesus, Mentoring, Tragedy, Trust.

Scriptures: Mark 1:16–20; 2:14; 8:34–36; 10:21; Luke 9:57–62; John 1:43; 10:1–6, 27; 21:22; 1 Corinthians 4:16; 11:1; Philippians 3:17; 2:5; 1 Thessalonians 1:6; 2:14; 2 Thessalonians 3:6, 9; Hebrews 12:1–3; 1 Peter 2:21; 1 John 2:6; 4:7–11.

84: Life

During the Second World War the island of Crete in the Mediterranean was invaded by the Nazis. As German paratroopers rained out of the sky onto the fields of Crete they were gunned down.

The retribution was terrible. The Germans lined up

whole villages of people and gunned them down. In the end hatred was the only weapon the Cretan people had. They vowed never to give up their hate. Never.

Yet today, on the site where the paratroopers landed, there is an institute where people come to learn about Greek culture and political harmony and peace. Why? Because of Dr Alexander Papaderos whose influence has changed his community. He is an exceptional human being.

During the War he was only a boy. One day, on the road, he found the broken pieces of a mirror. A German motor bike had crashed there. He tried to find all the pieces and reassemble the mirror, but he couldn't. So he kept the largest piece. By scratching it on a stone he made it round. He began to play with it as a toy. It became a game to reflect light into the most inaccessible places. Then Papaderos said this. 'I came to understand that this was not just a child's game but . . . what I might do with my life . . . I am a fragment of a mirror . . . I can reflect light into the dark places of this world'.

Themes: Darkness, Hatred, I am – the Light, Light, Reconciliation, Retribution, Salt and light, War.

Scriptures: Matthew 5:13–16; Mark 9:49–50; John 1:3–9; 3:19–21; 5:31–36; 8:12; 9:5; 11:9–10; 12:35–36; 12:46; Acts 13:47; 26:23; Romans 2:19; 1 Corinthians 4:5; 2 Corinthians 4:4–6; Ephesians 5:8, 13; 1 Thessalonians 5:5; 1 Peter 2:9; 2 Peter 1:19; 1 John 1:5; Revelation 21:23; 22:5.

85: Life

A voice came over the plane's sound system. 'We are climbing to our planned cruising altitude of 39,000 feet. All the plane's systems are working perfectly, and we expect to land in London on time. This is a fully automated plane. There is no pilot or co-pilot. Everything is guided and monitored by computer. We want you to sit back, relax and enjoy the flight. Nothing can go wrong . . . can go wrong . . . go wrong . . . go wrong . . .'

Themes: Deception, False messiahs, Humour, Tragedy, Sin.

Scriptures: Mark 13:22; Romans 1:18–32; 1 Corinthians 7:35; Galatians 6:9; 2 Peter 2:1; 1 John 4:1.

86: Life – storms

Victor Hugo wrote a story called *Ninety-Three*. In it he tells of a ship that was caught in a terrific storm. When the storm was at its height, the frightened crew heard a terrible crashing sound below deck. On investigation the source of the sound was discovered. A cannon they were carrying had broken loose. It was banging into the sides of the ship, tearing gaping holes in it with every smashing blow.

Risking their lives, two men went below. They managed to secure the cannon again. The captain and crew knew the loose cannon was more dangerous than the storm outside. The storm could toss them about, but the loose cannon within could be the means of sinking and destroying them.

Themes: Character, Gossip, Leadership, Loyalty, Negativity, Old nature, Storms, Temptation.

Scriptures: Mark 1:12–13; Luke 4:1–13; Romans 6:12–14; 2 Corinthians 12:1–13; Galatians 5:16–21; Ephesians 4:22; Colossians 3:8; James 1:2–4, 13–15, 21; 1 Peter 2:1.

87: Light

Some years ago a famous artist painted a picture. The painter lived where Christmas is in winter time. The scene was of a wintry and windy twilight. The white Christmas tree-shaped pines were bending under the force of the wind. In the middle of the dark picture the painter put a dreary, dull house. It seemed lonely and desolate in the midst of the cold scene. It was a sad picture. Then – as he was finishing the painting – with a quick stroke of the brush, he put a bright yellow light in one window. The picture was transformed. Now the scene seemed to be one of security and warmth.

Themes: Christmas, Darkness, Renewal, Security, Transformation, Warmth.

Scriptures: Matthew 5:13–16; Mark 9:49–50; John 1:3–9; 3:19–21; 5:31–36; 8:12; 9:5; 11:9–10; 12:35–36, 46; Acts 13:47; 26:23; Romans 2:19; 1 Corinthians 4:5; 2 Corinthians 4:4–6; Ephesians 5:8, 13; 1 Thessalonians 5:5; 1 Peter 2:9; 2 Peter 1:19; 1 John 1:5; Revelation 21:23; 22:5.

88: Love

Dr Griffith Evans of the Medical Research Council in England conducted experiments for twenty-five years with honeymoon couples, and injected the honeymoon couples with the virus of the common cold. But never once, throughout the twenty-five years of these experiments, did a honeymoon couple catch a cold. He came to the conclusion that, if there is real love and joy in the system, then this will protect the person against disease.

Themes: Anxiety, Healing, Illness, Joy, Marriage, Worry.

Scriptures: Proverbs 12:25; 15:13; 17:22; 1 John 4:18.

89: Love

A young lady in New England counted the days to the end of the Civil War when her fiancé would return. In the meantime she waited for letters. But they suddenly stopped. Eventually she received a letter in an unfamiliar hand. It read something like this: 'There has been another terrible battle. I have been unfortunate this time; I have lost both my arms. I cannot write myself, but my comrade is writing this letter for me. I write to tell you are as dear to me as ever; but I shall now be dependent upon other people for the rest of my days, and I have written this letter to release you from your engagement.' That letter was never answered. The young lady was on the next train and found her way to the hospital and eventually to her fiancé's bed. As in any good love story, she threw her arms around the soldier, 'I will never give you up', she said.

Themes: Acceptance, Parable – Prodigal Son, Reconciliation, War.

Scriptures: Proverbs 10:12; Luke 15:11–32; John 3:16; Romans 12:10; 1 Corinthians 13; 1 Thessalonians 4:9; 1 Peter 1:21; 4:8.

90: Love

Frank Higgins was a lumberjack and Christian leader. He was taken sick and plans were made to take him to the city hospital. The big fellows he had led to Christ held a consultation. They decided to send one of their number along with him to be of any service possible. For they loved the man who had taught them to love the Lord. The man chosen was a big, oversized fellow, decidedly out of place in the hospital. He stood around in the corridors waiting to be of some use to Frank. When the time came for the operation he said, 'Frank, you know we love you and want to help you. Now while the doctors are operating I will be at your door; and, Frank, if the doctors find that they need a quart of blood, or a piece of bone or skin, they can call on me. Frank, you can have every drop of blood or every bone in this body; now don't forget, I will be at the door.'

Themes: David and Jonathan, Friends, Jesus – work of, Sacrifice.

Scriptures: 1 Samuel 18:1–5; 19:1–8; John 3:16; 10:11–18; 13:1, 37; 15:13; Romans 5:7–8; 1 John 3:16; 4:9–10.

91: Love

Lorraine Hansberry wrote a play called *A raisin in the sun*. It is about a black family in Chicago's Southside. Walter, the son, loses the small family fortune in a bad deal. His sister pours out her contempt for his being so stupid. When she finishes her tirade, the mama speaks.

'. . . I thought I taught you to love him.'

'Love him?' the sister shouts back. 'There is nothing left to love.'

Then mama says, 'There is always something left to love. And if you ain't learnt that, you ain't learned nothing. Have you cried for that boy today? I don't mean for yourself and for the family 'cause we lost the money. I mean for him; what he been through and what it done to him. Child, when do you think is the time to love somebody the most; when they done good and made things easy for everybody? Well then, you ain't through learning – because that ain't the time at all. It's when he's at his lowest and can't believe in hisself 'cause the world done whipped him so.'

Themes: Materialism, Negativity, Parable – Prodigal Son, Parenting.

Scriptures: Proverbs 10:12; Luke 15:11–32; John 3.16; 10:11–18; 13:1, 37; 15:13; Romans 5:7–8; 12:10; 1 Corinthians 13; 1 Thessalonians 4:9; Hebrews 13:1; 1 Peter 1:22; 4:8; 1 John 3:16; 4:9–10.

92: Love

John Heinz is a paramedic. On one of his days off he was driving down a motorway near his home.

On the two-way radio he heard a call from someone to attend an emergency. A child had fallen from a tree and needed medical help immediately. John noted the address and saw that it was quite close to where he was. He took the next exit and made his way quickly to the house.

However, a couple of miles from the home he was stopped by some roadworks. An excavator was near completing a trench right across the road. John jumped out of his car. He hastily explained that he needed to get to a nearby house as there had been an accident. The excavator driver began quickly filling in the trench, just enough for John to be able to complete his mercy dash and attend to the child.

The next morning John was on his way to work and drove past the same excavator redigging the trench. John stopped to thank the driver for his cooperation. But as John got out of his car, the driver climbed out of his cabin and ran to John.

Before John could speak the man said, 'Oh, thank you, it was my child you saved yesterday.'

Themes: Atonement, Christmas, Easter, Evangelism, Family, God – his love, Rescue, Salvation.

Scriptures: Mark 10:45; Luke 4:18; 15:1–7, 8–10; 1 Corinthians 6:20; 7:23; 13; Galatians 4:4; Ephesians 2:11–21; 1 Timothy 2:5–6.

93: Love – practical

Steve Sjogren tells the story of Rictor. Rictor was going into a neighbourhood at Central Park Long Island giving away lightbulbs; knocking on doors and offering to show God's love in a practical way. Behind one door was a father and a son having a heated conversation. The son had come to Christ and was in a totally shark mode trying to corner his dad and talk him into coming to Christ. He was doing a pretty good job of getting his father's attention as well as irritating him. Dad had his hand on the doorknob ready to go to the shops. In his other hand was a shopping list he was waving at the lad saying, 'Son I'm not going to begin listening to what you Christians have to say until you begin to show the love of God instead of just talking about it all the time.' At that instant, as God would arrange it, the doorbell rang. 'What do you want?' the father said. Standing in front of him was a girl with a lightbulb in her hand saying, 'We would like to show you God's love in a practical way by giving you this lightbulb'. The first item on dad's shopping list was a lightbulb.

Themes: Christmas, Evangelism, Families, Fathers, Guidance, Servant Evangelism.

Scriptures: Psalms 25:9; 32:8; 48:14; Mark 3:7–12; 6:6–13; Luke 9:1–6; 10:1–20; Acts 1:8; 1 John 4:9–10.

94: Marriage

A young minister was having difficulty getting along with other people, especially his wife and family. He was continually criticizing her. Everything was wrong. He was sarcastic and demanding, and withdrew from her advances, rejecting her love and affection. He began to realize that he was destroying their marriage.

He went to talk and pray with anothe minister. Eventually the painful root of the matter came to light. While he was in the armed forces in Korea, he spent two weeks on leave in Japan. During that time, walking the streets of Tokyo, feeling empty, lonely, and terribly homesick, he fell into temptation and went three or four times to a prostitute. He had never been able to forgive himself. He had sought God's forgiveness, and with his *head*, believed he had it. But the guilt still plagued him and he hated himself. When he returned to his faithful fiancé his emotional conflicts increased because he still could not accept complete forgiveness. He felt he had no right to be happy. He said to himself, 'I have no right to enjoy my wife. I have no right to enjoy my life. I've got to pay back the debt.'

Themes: Forgiveness, Grace, Guilt, Inner healing, Pardon, Prayer, Prostitution.

Scriptures: 1 Kings 8:22–53; Psalms 51; 103:2–3; Jeremiah 31:34; Daniel 9; 19; Mark 2:1–12; 11:25; John 8:34–36; Romans 5; 6:23; Ephesians 2:8; 4:32; Colossians 2:13–14; 1 John 2:12.

95: Marriage

A little girl at play group heard the story of *Snow White* for the first time. She was so enthusiastic about the story she retold it at the tea table. After telling how the Prince had arrived on his white horse and kissed Snow White back to life she said, half asking, 'And do you know what happened then?'

'Of course', said her big brother, 'they lived happily ever after'.

'No they didn't', responded the girl, keen to tell the rest of the story herself, 'they got married.'

> **Themes:** Children, Contentment, Happiness, Humour, Husbands, Love, Wives.

> **Scriptures:** Deuteronomy 24:1–5; Matthew 5:27–29, 31–32; 19:3–12; Mark 10:2–12; Luke 10:27; John 14:15–24; Acts 5:29; 1 Corinthians 7:1–11; 13.

96: Marriage

A couple had just been married when the wife caught a bad cold. The husband put her to bed and called the doctor. Next winter she caught another cold. 'Maybe you had better lie down darling.' he said, 'nothing like a rest to fix a cold. I'll bring you something to eat. Have we got any soup?'

In their third year of marriage she got the usual cold.

This time he said, 'Look dear, be sensible. After you feed the baby and get the dishes done, you had better have a lie down.'

In the fourth year he said, as she coughed again and again, 'I wish you'd just gargle or something, instead of sitting around barking like a seal!'

In the fifth year of marriage and the next cold he said to her, 'For Pete's sake, stop sneezing! What are you trying to do, give us all pneumonia?'

Themes: Commitment, Compassion, Humour, Husbands, Kindness, Love, Sickness, Wives.

Scriptures: Deuteronomy 24:1–5; Matthew 5:27–29, 31–32; 19:3–12; Mark 10:2–12; Luke 10:27; John 14:15–24; Acts 5:29; 1 Corinthians 7:1–11; 13.

97: Marriage – renewed

The marriage of a Christian man was in a mess. He said this. 'It seemed that my wife and I were unable to communicate or relate on any level. I had fallen out of love with her – and to make it worse there was that other woman.'

Separation seemed the easy, almost desirable, way out. But God had different plans for them. Through the ministry of others who loved and supported them, they began to learn from God's Word that the only way forward with God is from the place of repentance and that total forgiveness of the past is a liberating experience. He went on to say something very interesting.

'I found that a lifetime of wrong attitudes and reactions had a binding effect on me. I needed long, patient counsel, culminating with prayers of authority, through which I experienced a physical release from a demonic deceit which had convinced me that what God wanted was not right. Now I praise God for insights given, power available and a renewed, revitalized and God-given marriage.'

Themes: Bible, Commitment, Communication, Demonic, Divorce, Inner healing, Love, Renewal, Separation.

Scriptures: Deuteronomy 24:1–5; Matthew 5:27–29, 31–32; 19:3–12; Mark 10:2–12; Luke 10:27; John 14:15–24; Acts 5:29; 1 Corinthians 7:1–11; 13.

98: Materialism

A person writing to the editor of *The Australian* newspaper had this to say:

> ... the real wealth creators and their contribution to Australia's prosperity should not only be recognised, it should be hailed as something to aspire to for all men and women ...
> It is not a sin to be rich. It is a fantastic achievement which should be hailed by all thinking people in the hope more people aspire to that status. Australia's leaders should openly promote the rewards of high achievement and should structure our tax to reward achievers *not* the non-achievers.

Themes: Achievement, Generosity, Greed, Lifestyle, Money, Prosperity, Purpose, Wealth.

Scriptures: Psalm 37:29; Proverbs 1:19; 15:27; 21:26; 29:25; Matthew 5:22; 6:24; Mark 4:18–19; 10:17–31; Luke 6:24; 12:16–21; 16:13, 19–31; Ephesians 4:28; 1 Timothy 3:3, 8; 6:10, 17–19.

99: Materialism

In an appeal for money, a piece of literature read as follows:

> There's no better way to insure your own financial security than to plant some seed-money in God's work. His law of sowing and reaping guarantees you a harvest of much more than you sow... Write on the enclosed slip what you need from God – the salvation of a loved one, healing, a raise in pay, a better job, newer car or home, sale or purchase of property, guidance in business investment... *whatever you need*... Enclose your slip with your seed-money... Expect God's material blessings in return...

Themes: Achievement, Generosity, Greed, Lifestyle, Money, Prosperity, Purpose, Wealth.

Scriptures: Psalm 37:29; Proverbs 1:19; 15:27; 21:26; 29:25; Malachi 3:8–10; Matthew 5:22; 6:24; Mark 4:18–19; 10:17–31; Luke 6:24; 12:16–21; 16:13, 19–31; Ephesians 4:28; 1 Timothy 3:3, 8; 6:10, 17–19.

100: Miracle

One Sunday Mr Alvarez went to church. He listened to a talk based on James 5. The preacher emphasized the need to pray for the sick and to anoint them with oil. How much of the message Mr Alvarez understood is unknown. He was not yet a Christian. The next morning, however, he awoke to find his most valuable bull was dead. This was a major tragedy. For a cowboy to lose his prize bull is like an admiral having his flagship sink. As he stared at his dead bull, Mr Alvarez remembered the talk he had heard the night before. He went into the kitchen. He got a can of olive oil. He then walked outside and anointed the immobile shape. He emptied the whole can over the animal. He also prayed. And the bull stood up and walked. When Mr Alvarez told Ed Silvoso about the bull, Ed was somewhat sceptical. Silvoso made the mistake of questioning Mr Alavrez. Mr Alvarez took off his glasses and looked Ed straight in the eye. With a booming voice he said, 'Young man, I have been a cowboy for over half a century. I know cows and bulls inside out. If I tell you it was dead, it was dead! Understood?' Not surprisingly, Mr Alvarez became a Christian.

Themes: Conversion, Doubt, Faith, Healing, Humour, Prayer, Signs and wonders, Trust.

Scriptures: Psalm 37:3-5; Proverbs 3:5-6; Matthew 8:5-13; 9:27-31; Mark 1:29-31, 40-44; 2:1-12; 3:1-6; 5:24-34; 7:31-37; 8:22-26; 10:46-52; 11:22-24; Luke 7:1-10; 13:10-17; 14:1-6; John 4:46-54; 9:1-34; James 5:14-15.

101: Mission – cost

It is 25 May 1961. The forty-three-year-old President John F Kennedy stands before the joint session of Congress to deliver his dramatic challenge to Americans. He speaks in his crisp New England accent and jabbing the air with his forefinger for emphasis. This is what he says: 'I believe that this nation should commit itself to achieving the goal, before the decade is out, of landing a man on the moon and returning him safely to earth. No single space project in this period will be more impressive to mankind, or more important for the long-range exploration of space; and none will be so difficult or expensive to accomplish ... In a very real sense, it will not be one man going to the moon ... it will be an entire nation. For all of us must work to put him there ... I believe we should go to the moon ... Unless we are prepared to do the work and bear the burdens to make it successful, there is no sense in going ahead.'

At the conclusion of Kennedy's forty-seven-minute message there was only routine applause. As he left the Congress, members were split over his proposal to spend $40 billion in the decade ahead in the mission to put a man on the moon. But Kennedy turned out to have been successful. The race to the moon had begun. Millions and millions of dollars poured into the programme. In a few years in the mid 60s over $15 billion a year was being spent on the mission. Men and women from all over America were recruited to join the programme. There were scientists, technical support personnel, people with trades and crafts, clerks and administrators. The best people were giving their best. For one scientist it was so exhilarating he said he would have worked for nothing if he could have afforded it. At one stage NASA was employing 36,000 people in the mission to put a man on the moon. There were another 300,000 sub-contractors dedicated to the task.

Eight years after Kennedy's challenge, Buzz Aldrin and Neil Armstrong were descending towards the moon in the Eagle. It was 20 July 1969. A quarter of a million miles away Charlie Drake called from Mission Control. 'If you read, you're go for powered descent.' Neil said his instrument panel was alive with winking data. Unexpectedly an alarm went off. The computer couldn't cope with all the data. Buzz and Neil eyed the large red ABORT button. But the guidance officers at mission control called that it was an acceptable risk. 500 feet above the surface Neil Armstrong took manual control. He wasn't satisfied with the landing zone. He delicately stroked the hand controller. They scooted horizontally across a field of rubbly boulders. They were now short of fuel. They would have to land or abort in sixty seconds. At thirty seconds Neil was still hovering. At twenty seconds they settled silently on the moon. 'Houston', Neil called, 'Tranquility Base here. The Eagle has landed.' Buzz reached across and shook Neil's hand, hard. They had pulled it off.

It took several hours to suit up for the moon walk. They depressurised the module. Neil opened the hatch. Buzz guided him as he backed out on his hands and knees. When he reached the ladder he moved down carefully. 'I'm at the foot of the ladder,' Neil said. His voice was low and precise. 'I'm going to step off the Lunar Module now...' Through his window Buzz watched Neil. He could see Neil move his blue lunar overshoe from the metal dish of the foot pad to the powdery grey surface. 'That's one small step for ... man, one giant leap for mankind.' Around the world, millions and millions of people stopped to watch the television screen following the success of one of the greatest human missions of all time. And, hundreds of billions of dollars, hundreds of thousands of people had worked to make that mission possible.

Themes: Christmas, Evangelism, Incarnation, Purpose.

Scriptures: Isaiah 9:6–7; 11:1–3; Jeremiah 23:5–6; Micah 5:2; Matthew 1:18–25; 28:18–20; Mark 1:1–3; 3:13–15; 6:7–13; Luke 1:26–2:20; 9:1–6; 10:1–20; John 1:1–18; 3:17; Acts 1:8; 13:22–23; Romans 1:3; 8:3; 2 Corinthians 8; 9; Galatians 4:4–5; 1 Timothy 1:15; Hebrews 1:1–14; 2:9–18; 10:4–14; 1 John 2:22; 4:2–3; 2 John 7.

102: Money

On the weekend of 13–14 February 1993, a man unnamed in press reports was heading for Toulouse on a TGV high-speed train. The train's lavatory had a voracious drainage system which swallowed the man's wallet with a triumphant snap as he was bending to adjust his clothing. As the man tried to retrieve his wallet, the loo's jaws clamped savagely round his wrist. Somehow, he managed to pull the alarm and the train screeched to a halt near Tours. Firemen had to destroy the vicious appliance with metal cutters. France's television viewers saw the unfortunate traveller being carried away on a stretcher, his wallet in one hand and the lavatory bowl still wrapped around his wrist.

Themes: Humour, Materialism, Poverty, Riches, Wealth.

Scriptures: Psalm 37:29; Proverbs 1:19; 15:27; 21:26; 29:25; Matthew 5:22; 6:24; Mark 4:18–19; 10:17–31; Luke 6:24; 12:16–21; 16:13, 19–31; Ephesians 4:28; 1 Timothy 3:3, 8; 6:10, 17–19.

103: Negativity

In the late 1600s the French and the English were at war which involved fighting in the colonies in Canada. Sir William Phips was put in charge of the British naval attack on Quebec. Sir William had arranged to wait offshore until Major Walley had led some men around the rear of the town. But Sir William became impatient of waiting. He started to fire on the city.

The Catholic French of Quebec had hung a massive picture of the Holy Family on the spire of the Cathedral. They were hoping it would increase divine aid for their cause. Protestant Sir William was not impressed. It then seemed that every gun on his ships was trained on the Cathedral spire. Volley after volley was poured on to that picture. But still it hung there. Meanwhile, Sir William had forgotten about Major Walley. Walley and his men became in great need of food and other supplies. Phips had spent so much of his time and ammunition firing at the saints that he could no longer help Major Walley. Also, he did not have enough ammunition left to fire at the enemy in the ensuing battle, which he lost because he had been firing at the saints.

Themes: Enemies, Evil, Good, Life, New life, Old life, Spiritual battle.

Scriptures: Psalm 1; Romans 6:1–14; 7:14–23; 8:31–39; 1 Corinthians 4:16; 9:24–27; 16:13; 2 Corinthians 10:1–6; Galatians 5:16–26; Ephesians 3:16–17; 4:17–5:2; 6:10–20; Colossians 3:1–17; 1 Timothy 1:18.

104: *New life*

Chester Szuber lives in Berkeley, Michigan. Chester and his wife have six children. The youngest, Patti, was twenty-two. Chester had suffered three open heart operations and, in August 1994, had been waiting four years for a heart transplant. Without a new heart his life would soon be over.

In August 1994, tragedy struck. While Chester was waiting for a new heart, his daughter Patti was involved in a serious car accident. Patti was rushed to hospital. The family experienced four excruciating days hovering around the intensive care unit. Sadly Patti's brain stopped functioning. Then the family was faced with a momentous decision which resulted in a wonderful resolution to this tragedy. Before her fatal accident, Patti had signed an organ donor card. She wanted the suitable organs of her body to be used to give life to others. The family had long discussions with a counsellor and members of the medical team. The family decided Patti would have wanted her heart to be given to her father, who desperately needed it.

The medical team worked quickly. Patti's heart was taken from her lifeless body and flown to Michigan. Her dad was already in surgery with another medical team waiting. His daughter's heart was stitched into place. With tension rising in the operating theatre, the team watched the new heart start inside Chester.

Patti's brother, Bob, said his sister must be the 'happiest angel in heaven'.

Themes: Atonement, Cross, Grief, Jesus – work of, Love, Sacrifice, Salvation, Substitution, Suffering.

Scriptures: Psalm 27:14; Isaiah 53; Mark 10:45; Luke 10:27; John 11:50; Romans 3:21–25; 1 Corinthians 13; Galatians 3:13; 1 Timothy 2:6; Hebrews 9:28; 1 Peter 2:24.

105: Obedience

En route to the African Crusades in 1960, Leighton Ford stopped briefly at Dakar, West Africa. A French missionary of the Reformed Church met him for coffee. He had laboured in that Muslim centre for ten years. One of the group with Leighton Ford asked,

'How many converts have you had?'

'Oh', he thought, 'one, two – perhaps three'.

'Three converts in ten years! Why do you stay?'

'Why do I stay?'

His face mirrored his surprise at the thoughtless question.

'I stay because Jesus Christ put me here!'

Themes: Call, Church growth, Conversion, Failure, Missionaries, Perseverance, Success.

Scriptures: Genesis 22:18; 1 Samuel 15:22; Jeremiah 7:22–23; 20:9; John 6:29; 14:15–24; Acts 5:29; 6:7; Romans 5:19; 6:17; 9:31–10:3, 16; 12:1–2; 1 Corinthians 15:22; Galatians 2:20; Ephesians 4:32–5:2; Philippians 2:5–8; 2 Thessalonians 1:8; Titus 2:14; Hebrews 5:8–9; 11:8, 17; 1 Peter 1:15–16, 22; 2:8; 3:1; 4:2, 17; 1 John 3:23.

106: Obedience

Communists demand total obedience of their members. An American student wrote a letter to his fiancée breaking off his engagement.

> We communists . . . get shot at, hung, jailed, lynched, tarred and feathered, slandered, ridiculed, and fired from our jobs, and in every other way made uncomfortable. A certain percentage of us gets killed or imprisoned; we live in virtual poverty. We turn back to the Party every penny we make above what is necessary to keep alive. We communists don't have the time or money for many movies or concerts or T-bone steaks or decent homes or new cars. We've been described as fanatics; we are fanatics. Our lives are dominated by one overshadowing factor: the Struggle for World Communism! We communists have a philosophy of life which no amount of money could buy. We have a cause to fight for, a definite purpose in life. We subordinate our petty personal selves into a great movement for humanity. There is one thing about which I am in earnest: the communist

cause! It is my life, my business, my religion, my hobby, my sweetheart, my wife, my mistress, my bread and my meat! I work at it in the daytime and dream of it at night! Therefore I cannot carry on a friendship, a love affair, or even a conversation, without relating everything to this force which both guides and drives my life ... I have already been in jail because of my ideas, and if necessary I am ready to go before a firing squad.

Themes: Goals, Humility, Jesus – character, Life, Perseverance, Purpose, Submission, Suffering, Vision.

Scriptures: Genesis 22:18; 1 Samuel 15:22; Jeremiah 7:22–23; 20:9; John 6:29; 14:15–24; Acts 5:29; 6:7; Romans 5:19; 6:17; 9:31–10:3, 16; 12:1–2; 1 Corinthians 15:22; Galatians 2:20; Ephesians 4:32–5:2; Philippians 2:5–8; 2 Thessalonians 1:8; Titus 2:14; Hebrews 5:8–9; 11:8, 17; 1 Peter 1:15–16, 22; 2:8; 3:1; 4:2, 17; 1 John 3:23.

107: Obedience

Bishop Thomas Coke, famed as one of the founders of Methodism in America, crossed the Atlantic nine times in the line of duty. At the age of sixty-seven he felt called by God to go to India and establish Wesleyan Missions. When a friend questioned his sense Coke replied; 'I am now dead to Europe and alive for India. God has said to me, "Go to Ceylon". I would rather be set naked on its coast and without a friend than not go.'

Themes: Missionaries, Old age.

Scriptures: Genesis 22:18; 1 Samuel 15:22; Jeremiah 7:22–23; 20:9; John 6:29; 14:15–24; Acts 5:29; 6:7; Romans 5:19; 6:17; 9:31–10:3, 16; 12:1–2; 1 Corinthians 15:22; Galatians 2:20; Ephesians 4:32–5:2; Philippians 2:5–8; 2 Thessalonians 1:8; Titus 2:14; Hebrews 5:8–9; 11:8, 17; 1 Peter 1:15–16, 22; 2:8; 3:1; 4:2, 17; 1 John 3:23.

108: Occult

A young man was being counselled by a minister as he was emerging from a homosexual affair and was seeking to get his life back into order with Jesus. Something still seemed to be holding him back. During the time of prayer he happened to mention a ring which his former partner had given him as a mark of their relationship and which he was still wearing. It turned out that this ring had been charmed by a medium. The ring was immediately removed and given up. He repented again of his former lifestyle and renounced the ring and all it stood for. From that time onwards he noticed an immediate release and knew he was free from what had held him back in his spiritual growth.

Themes: Demonic, Freedom, Homosexuality, Magic, Repentance.

Scriptures: Exodus 22:20; 32:8; 34:15; Leviticus 18:26, 31; Deuteronomy 18:10–13; 32:17; Luke 4:18; Acts 19:11–20; Romans 8:31–39.

109: Optimism

A family had two primary school aged children. One of the lads was always grumpy and complaining – a real pessimist. The other was always bright and cheerful and could never see anything wrong with anything – a real optimist. The parents were a bit worried about how they would end up coping in life. One Saturday, the father decided to purchase every popular toy he could lay his hands on. He gave them to the grumpy pessimistic child. He also had a truck load of manure up-ended in the shed for the optimist. Saturday afternoon, the parents found the pessimistic son sitting in his room sobbing away because he was afraid he would break the toys if he played with them. When they went out to the shed, there was the optimistic fellow having a great time burrowing around in the pile of manure. 'What are you doing?' the dad asked. 'Oh dad, I just know there's a horse in here somewhere.'

Themes: Humour, Life, Parenting, Pessimism, Positive, Praise, Thanksgiving.

Scriptures: Genesis 18:19; Deuteronomy 5:16; 6:4–9; Psalms 34:1; 71:6; Hosea 14:2; Ephesians 5:20; 6:1, 4; Colossians 3:20–21; Hebrews 13:15; 1 Peter 2:5.

110: Parenting

There was a man who seemed to have a built-in slave driver. As a boy he sought to please his parents. He would set the table, but either he would put the knives in the wrong place or the forks up the wrong way. When he came home with a report full of C's his parents wanted him to get B's. When he came home with B's his parents said he ought to get A's. When he got A's his Dad said, 'Well, I know those teachers. They always give A's.' He collapsed under the strain.

> **Themes:** Barnabas, Children, Discouragement, Encouragement, Failure, Families, Fathers, Stress, Success.
>
> **Scriptures:** Genesis 18:19; Deuteronomy 5:16; 6:4–9; Acts 4:36; Ephesians 6:1, 4; Philippians 2:1; Colossians 3:20–21; 1 Thessalonians 2:12; 5:14.

111: Parenting

Steve Martin and Mary Steenburgen star in the comedy film *Parenthood*. It is a message to parents that childbearing is a life sentence to anxiety. In one scene the counsellor is talking to the parents about their Kevin and says, 'You should not look on the fact that Kevin will be going to a special school as any kind of failure on your part.'

'Right', says Dad, 'I'll blame the dog.'

Themes: Children, Fathers, Humour, Mothers.

Scriptures: Genesis 18:19; Deuteronomy 5:16; 6:4–9; Ephesians 6:1, 4; Colossians 3:20–21.

112: Parenting

A mother of a rebellious thirteen-year-old boy, who was totally beyond her parental authority, sought help from a Christian professor of child development. The lad would not come home until 2.00 am or later. He disobeyed every request she made of him. The psychologist asked if she could tell him the history of the problem. She said that she could clearly remember when it all started. Her son was less than three at the time. She carried him to his room and placed him in his bed. He spat in her face to demonstrate his usual bedtime attitude. She attempted to explain the importance of not spitting in her face. But her lecture was interrupted by another moist missile. This mother had been told that all confrontation could be resolved by love and understanding and discussion. She wiped her face and began again. At which point the youngster hit her with another well-aimed blast. She began to get frustrated and shook him. But not hard enough to throw off his aim of his next contribution. What could she do? Her philosophy of becoming a parent offered no honourable solution. Finally, she rushed from the room in utter exasperation. And her little conqueror spat on the back of the door as it shut. She lost; he won! She said she never had the upper hand with her child after that night.

Themes: Children, Fathers, Humour, Mothers.

Scriptures: Genesis 18:19; Deuteronomy 5:16; 6:4–9; Ephesians 6:1, 4; Colossians 3:20–21.

113: Parenting

A father had reached a brick wall with Bob, his seventeen-year-old son who had been stealing. One day, when the evidence was incontrovertible, the father was overwhelmed with rage with God. He said, 'I told God I hated Bob. I told him I could take no more. I asked him either to kill me or to kill the boy – I'd really reached the limit. I'd done everything I could, disciplined firmly and consistently, been understanding, established a good rapport with the boy. For years, I'd put up with court appearances, family therapy from psychiatrists, crisis after crisis . . . I don't know what happened to me or why I reacted so strongly, but inside me all hell broke loose.' Then the father said that something had dawned on him. He realized his discipline was always to control something in Bob's life. It had never occurred to him to punish Bob because justice demanded punishment. The dad said, at this point, he felt scared, for he realized justice would mean a stick to Bob's rear end. Bob was now bigger and stronger than his dad – and a fight would be a disaster. The father was a Christian and he prayed about it for hours. Eventually he felt at peace and was able to tell Bob he had to be punished for what he had done wrong. To his surprise and relief, his son accepted it like a lamb. The father said later, 'Something happened. It had nothing to do with the physical part but the simple business of coming to terms with justice. He's never been the same since.' He went on to say that a great change happened to him too, as he realized he had been more worried about his pride than about his son knowing justice and logical consequences in his life.

Themes: Control, Discipline, Fathers, Justice, Punishment, Theft.

Scriptures: Genesis 18:19; Deuteronomy 5:16, 19; 6:4–9; Ephesians 6:1, 4; Colossians 3:20–21.

114: Parenting

Jim Cymbala is a minister in Brooklyn New York. He has been there now for twenty-one years. Jim and his wife Carol have three children.

Up to the age of sixteen, Chrissy, their oldest daughter, was a model child. But, then, she drifted away from God. She became involved with a young man who was not a Christian, and eventually she moved out of home and became pregnant.

Jim, and Carol went through a dark tunnel of two-and-a-half-years. On Sundays, as he went off to preach, Jim would often cry from the minute he left the house until he got to the church door.

After Chrissy had been away for two years Jim spent time in Florida. As he prayed he said to God, 'I've been battling, crying, screaming, arguing, and manoeuvring with Chrissy. No more arguing, no more talking. It's just you and me. I'm just going to pray for my daughter.'

Four months later, on a Tuesday in February, Jim was in the church prayer meeting. Someone passed him a note. It said this person felt deeply impressed that they should stop the meeting and pray for his daughter. Jim struggled to know if this was right.

At that moment, Chrissy was at a friend's home somewhere in Brooklyn, with her baby.

Jim decided to interrupt the meeting. He told the people his daughter was confused and in a mess. She thought up was down, white was black, and black was white. Jim said the room soon felt like the labour room in a hospital. The people called out to God with incredible intensity. When he got home he told Carol that something had happened in heavenly places.

Thirty-six hours later, Jim was standing in the bathroom shaving. Carol burst in, 'Chrissy's here, you better go downstairs.'

'I don't know . . .' he said.

'Trust me. Go downstairs,' Carol said.

Jim wiped off the shaving cream. He went down to the kitchen and there was his daughter, nineteen years old, and on her knees weeping. She grabbed his leg and said, 'Dad, I've sinned against God. I've sinned against you. I've sinned against myself.'

Sobbing and sniffing, Chrissy went on to explain that God had woken her in the middle of Tuesday night. God showed her that she was heading towards a pit, a chasm, and she was so afraid. Then she said that God showed her that he hadn't given up on her.

As Jim looked into the face of his daughter he saw again the girl they had raised. Chrissy and their granddaughter moved in with Jim and Carol.

That was five years ago. Today, Chrissy is the music director in the church, and in the last three-and-a-half years she has married.

> **Themes:** Anxiety, Confession, Fathers, Parable – Prodigal Son, Prayer, Reconciliation, Repentance.

> **Scriptures:** Matthew 6:25; Mark 1:15; Luke 12:22–31; 15:11–32; Ephesians 6:18; Philippians 4:6.

115: Persecution

Iosyp Terelya, a Catholic born in 1943, wrote to his friends at Christmas 1981:

> Dear Brothers and Sisters,
> Another year of captivity has passed. Thank God, I again see the dear and familiar faces of friends and family, of my little children and my beloved wife. We live on earth in order to praise God . . . The entire life of a Christian is the cross and martyrdom, if he wants to live according to the Gospel.

In May 1983 a Father Svarinskas was sentenced to seven years in a strict-regime camp and three years in internal exile on charges of slandering the Soviet State. He wrote a personal account of his trial in a letter. At the end he said:

> God has provided for me the fate of the martyrs. Therefore, it only remains for me to show myself worthy of the grace of God. These ten years of want and suffering will be the crown of my priesthood. Let us pray for one another, so that we do not crumble under the cross of the Lord.

Themes: Martyrs, Persistence, Praise, Suffering.

Scriptures: Psalms 34:1; 71:6; Hosea 14:2; Matthew 5:12; Romans 5:3–5; 14:7–8; 2 Corinthians 5:15; Galatians 2:20; 6:9; Ephesians 5:20; Philippians 1:21; 4:12; Hebrews 10:34; 13:15; James 1:2–4; 1 Peter 1:7; 2:5.

116: Persistence

Samuel Taylor Coleridge (1772–1834) was a great British poet and critic. But he could have been even greater. He left Cambridge University to join the army. He left the army because he could not rub down a horse. He returned to Oxford and left without a degree. He began a paper called *The Watchman*. But it failed after ten issues. It has been said of him, 'He lost himself in visions of work to be done, but it always remained to be done.'

It was said of Coleridge that he had every poetic gift but one – the gift of sustained and concentrated effort. In his head were all kinds of ideas. He told friends his work was: '. . . completed save for transcriptions. I am on the eve of sending to the press two Octavo volumes.' But his work rarely came to anything outside his mind.

Themes: Creativity, Failure, Good works, Laziness.

Scriptures: Matthew 5:14–16; 2 Corinthians 9:8; Galatians 6:9; Ephesians 2:1–10; Colossians 1:10; 2 Timothy 2:21; Titus 2:14; 3:1.

117: Pornography

Ted Bundy was a serial killer. He killed thirty-one women throughout the US. In the hours before he went to the electric chair in 1989, he issued a chilling warning on the dangers of violent pornography. He said this: 'Those of us who have been influenced by violence in the media, in particular pornographic violence, are not some kind of inherent monsters. We are your sons, your husbands.' He also said, 'Lots of other kids playing the streets around this country today are going to be dead tomorrow and the next day and next month because other young people are reading the kinds of things and seeing the kinds of things available in the media today . . . You keep craving something that is harder and gives you a greater sense of excitement until you reach a point where the pornography only goes so far and you wonder whether actually doing it will give you that which is beyond just reading about it and looking at it.'

He claimed that as a boy of thirteen or fourteen he encountered 'soft core' porn in local stores. 'I want to emphasise,' he said, 'this is the most damaging kind of pornography.'

Bundy, once a law student and Republican Party worker, said he grew up in a 'wonderful home with two dedicated and loving parents.' He said, 'It was a fine, solid Christian home and I hope no one will try to take the easy way and try to blame or otherwise accuse my family of contributing to this.'

Themes: Capital punishment, Media, Murder, Parenting, Purity, Violence.

Scriptures: Genesis 18:19; Deuteronomy 5:16; 6:4–9; Matthew 5:27–30; Romans 7:14–23; Ephesians 6:1, 4; Philippians 4:8; Colossians 3:20–21.

118: Power

The Darwin Award is an annual honour given by forensic scientists to 'a dim witted person who has done the human gene pool a great service by killing himself in an extraordinarily stupid way'. In 1995 it was awarded to a man in Arizona.

In Arizona a police patrol came across a pile of smouldering metal pressed into a cliff. The cliff was at the apex of a tight curve in a two lane highway. It looked like an aircraft crash site. But it turned out to be a car. Forensic scientists were called in to reconstruct what had happened. The award winner had got hold of an airforce JATO. A JATO is a jet assisted take-off solid fuel rocket. It is sometimes attached to military transport planes taking off from short airfields. The Darwin Award winner had driven his Chevy Impala into the Arizona desert and found a long straight stretch of road. He attached the JATO to the rear of his Chevy. He jumped in, got up speed and then fired up the rocket. Once a JATO is switched on it cannot be switched off; it simply burns until all the fuel has gone . . .

As far as can be determined, he was travelling somewhere between 450 and 500 kph when he came to the curve in the road.

Themes: 'Dunamis', Direction, Energy, Holy Spirit, Humour, Resurrection.

Scriptures: Acts 1:8; 4:7, 14, 33; 5:17; 6:8; 10:38; Romans 1:16; 1 Corinthians 1:18; 9:23–27; Ephesians 1:19–20; Philippians 3:10; 2 Timothy 1:7–8.

119: Practicalities

G K Chesterton was a British novelist and journalist in the early years of the twentieth century. He and several literary friends gathered one evening to enjoy some stimulating intellectual conversation. One of them posed a hypothetical question: 'If you were isolated on a desert island and could have only one book, what volume would you choose?'

Not surprisingly, one guest replied, 'The complete works of Shakespeare.' Another, of course, said, 'I'd choose the Bible.'

When Chesterton's turn came, he gave a different kind of answer. He said, 'I would choose *Thomas' Guide to Practical Shipbuilding.*'

Themes: Bible, Decisions, Humour, Priorities.

Scriptures: Mark 14:25–43; 2 Timothy 3:16–17.

120: Praise

When Richard Wurmbrand was in communist prisons for fourteen years, three of them in solitary confinement thirty feet below ground level, he learnt to praise God as an act of sheer obedience. As he continued to do so, he discovered a beauty in Christ he had never known before. He also experienced visions of heaven, and those visions helped to sustain his life in the most extreme circumstances.

Themes: Obedience, Persecution, Suffering, Visions.

Scriptures: Psalms 34:1; 71:6; Joel 2:28; Matthew 5:12; Acts 2:17; Romans 5:3–5; Ephesians 5:20; Philippians 4:12; Hebrews 10:34; 13:15; James 1:2–4; 1 Peter 1:6–7; 2:5.

121: Prayer

I heard the sad story of a missionary, his wife and three children who went to the Far East. Before they left home their local church gave them full assurance that folk would support them financially and pray for them. In order to help the folk pray intelligently the missionary family sent back tapes and letters telling of their news and needs. Unbeknown to the missionary family, there was only one person in the church family who showed any ongoing interest in them. The missionary adventure turned to disaster. The husband had a great deal of difficulty learning the languages. There was great opposition from the government and non-Christian forces in the country. Then tragically, at the age of only twenty-six, the wife contracted Blackwater fever. After a short time she died, leaving him with the three children. He stayed on and completed his first term. When he went home to his church family he was keen to get to the prayer meeting. They prayed for the Sunday School picnic, the new building programme and the women's trip to a conference. The young missionary sat stunned in the back row. At the end of the meeting the minister approached him. The first thing the missionary said was, 'Now I understand. This is the reason.'

'What on earth are you talking about?' asked the minister. 'Those years on the field,' said the missionary. 'The difficulties, the pain, the lack of results. This is the reason.'

Themes: Faithfulness, Intercession, Missionaries, Prayer – answered.

Scriptures: Romans 1:8–12; 12:12; 1 Corinthians 14:14–16; Ephesians 1:15–19; 3:14–18; 6:13–18; Philippians 4:6; Colossians 1:9–14; 4:2; 1 Thessalonians 1:2.

122: Prayer

In 1727 the Moravian church was part of the Lutheran church in Germany. The Moravians were deeply divided, people were critical of each other and they argued about everything. Their leader, Count Zinzendorf, pleaded for love and unity. On 5 August he spent the whole night in prayer with about twelve or fourteen others. On Sunday, 10 August, about midday, the whole congregation was overwhelmed with the powerful presence of God. They continued until midnight in prayer, singing, weeping and praying. Also, the children in the church were touched by God and began to hold their own prayer meetings. On 26 August, twenty-four men and twenty-four women agreed to continue praying around the clock, taking an hour each. On 27 August, they agreed on a weekly meeting where prayer needs would be given out. As a direct result of prayer for God's filling of their lives with the Holy Spirit, the Moravian church sent out over 100 missionaries in just two decades.

Themes: God – presence of, Intercession, Missionaries, Prayer – answered, Prayer – constant, Prayer – vigil, Revival, Toronto Blessing.

Scriptures: Acts 4:30–31; Romans 1:8–12; 12:12; 1 Corinthians 14:14–16; Ephesians 1:15–19; 3:14–18; 6:13–18; Philippians 4:6; Colossians 1:9–14; 4:2; 1 Thessalonians 1:2; 5:17.

123: Prayer – answers

The Irish Evangelist, Derick Bingham, had a deep urge to become involved in children's literature. He needed £250 for the project. He prayed about it. One afternoon he was with a friend who said, 'Is there any work for the Lord in which you are involved at the moment which needs some money?' Derick was a bit embarrassed, but his friend coaxed him along saying that he and his wife had been praying this particular day and been told to offer him some money. Derick admitted that he was producing some booklets on the gospel for children that would cost £250. Drawing an envelope from his pocket, and with tears in his eyes, his friend laid the little packet on the table. 'Inside you will find £250 exactly,' he said.

Themes: Evangelism, Giving, God's provision, Miracles.

Scriptures: Psalm 112:9; Isaiah 55:10; Mark 10:17–31; 11:22–24; 12:41–44; Luke 7:1–10; 19:1–10; Romans 1:8–12; 12:12; 1 Corinthians 14:14–16; 2 Corinthians 8; 9; Ephesians 1:15–19; 3:14–18; 6:13–18; Philippians 4:6; Colossians 1:9–14; 4:2; 1 Thessalonians 1:2; 1 Timothy 6:17–19; Hebrews 13:5.

124: Prayer and fasting

Minnesota farmers know locust plagues well. Their crops had been destroyed by the voraciously hungry insects in the summer of 1876.

In the spring of 1877 they waited and watched to see whether or not such pestilence would strike yet again.

If it did, the farming future of families would be wiped out permanently.

Acutely aware of the impending disaster, Governor J S Pillsbury proclaimed that 26 April would be a day of prayer and fasting to plead with God to save them from calamity.

The Governor urged that every single person should unite and participate toward this end.

Across the state people responded to their Governor's call. In gatherings large and small, Minnesotans assembled to fast and pray.

The next day, as the sun soared in a cloudless sky, with temperatures also rising, the people noticed to their dismay that the dreaded insects started to stir in the warmed soil.

For three days the uninterrupted unseasonal heat caused a vast army of locusts to hatch. It was of such plague proportions as to threaten the entire north-west farm sector.

Then, as the sun departed at the end of the fourth day, there was a sudden climatic change. A blanket of frost flicked across the entire area where the locusts waited for dawn and take-off. Most were killed right where they crouched.

Come summer, instead of scorched stubbled dirt, as far as the eye could see, the wheat crop waved in golden glory.

In the history of Minnesota, 26 April 1877 is recorded as the day when God wonderfully responded to the prayers and fasting of his people.

Themes: Fasting, Miracles, Prayer – answered, Prayer – vigil.

Scriptures: Exodus 34:27–28; 2 Samuel 12:16–24; Ezra 8:21; Psalm 69:10; Isaiah 58:5–12; Jeremiah 14:11–12; Zechariah 7:1–14; 8:19; Mark 2:18–22; Romans 1:8–12; 12:12; 1 Corinthians 14:14–16; Ephesians 1:15–19; 3:14–18; 6:13–18; Philippians 4:6; Colossians 1:9–14; 4:2; 1 Thessalonians 1:2.

125: Prayer and fasting

In a south Asian city a western missionary saw a cow about to be slaughtered in front of a mosque during the Muslim festival of Eid ul Adha. He stopped his car, took a few pictures, then drove home.

But that night the Holy Spirit began to challenge him to be less a tourist and more a missionary. He was directed to start praying and fasting. To return to the scene of the sacrifice and to be a witness to the greater sacrifice of Jesus.

In the steaming pre-monsoon heat of the next day, he set off with his shoulder bag full of tracts and gospels to the same place in the bazaar, near the mosque.

Having sold and distributed much literature, he felt well satisfied as he returned home that he had done his 'duty'. But the Holy Spirit impressed upon him that night that he was to continue his praying and fasting and to return to repeat the process in the same place the next day.

Night after night, as the missionary prayed, the Holy Spirit repeated his instruction to his obedient servant.

It didn't take long for local opposition to form and even threaten his life.

He was dragged through the market place, doused in dye, kicked and pushed into a ditch and stoned.

Twice a fanatic tried to kill him with a dagger but was restrained by his own people.

Finally, two well-trained rabble-rousers were appointed to stop his witnessing. They approached him directly, warning him that, should he return again, he wouldn't leave the bazaar alive.

On the 40th day of this supernaturally sustained period of prayer and fasting, directed by what the Spirit was saying, he bade farewell to his wife for what he thought could be the last time. He set out once more with his literature to sell and distribute in the bazaar. No sooner had he arrived than the appointed 'crowd conductors' also showed up. They tore up his gospels and his tracts and began to incite the growing crowd to watch the spectacle. Soon there were calls to kill him.

Then, as men moved in to grab him, two unusually tall strangers appeared.

Spearing a path through the crowd which was now calling for the missionary's blood, they grabbed him, in one swift move, removed him from the crush of people and took him down an alleyway at the end of which was a waiting bicycle rickshaw.

Amazingly, no one had followed them.

Placing the missionary in the rickshaw, the strangers said to him, 'It is enough now. Don't come back.' God's messengers had saved his servant.

That night the Lord spoke once more saying, 'Now you know how much I love and care for Muslims. It is not my will that any of them should perish without hearing the message of salvation.'

With no other tangible resources, other than the practice of sustained prayer and fasting, that missionary went on to be used by God to build what became one of the largest churches in that hostile environment.

Themes: Angels, Church growth, Fasting, Guidance, Holy Spirit – directing, Miracles, Missionaries, Persecution.

Scriptures: Exodus 34:27–28; 2 Samuel 12:16–24; Ezra 8:21; Psalm 69:10; Isaiah 58:5–12; Jeremiah 14:11–12; Zechariah 7:1–14; 8:19; Mark 2:18–22; John 14:26; 16:12–13; Acts 8:1–40; 13:1–3; 16:7; Romans 1:8–12; 12:12; 1 Corinthians 14:14–16; Ephesians 1:15–19; 3:14–18; 6:13–18; Philippians 4:6; Colossians 1:9–14; 4:2; 1 Thessalonians 1:2; 1 John 2:27.

126: Prayer – persistence

Two African chiefs came to Chalmers the missionary. They asked for Christian teachers for their villages but Chalmers apologized saying he did not have anyone to send. Two years went by. Chalmers decided to go himself when the chiefs returned to pester him again. When he arrived in one of the villages, he was surprised by what he saw. It was Sunday and all the people were on their knees, in perfect silence. Chalmers asked the chief, 'What are you doing?'

'We are praying,' he said.

'But you are not saying anything,' Chalmers returned.

The chief then said, 'White man, we do not know what to say. For two years, every Sunday morning we have met here. And for four hours we have been on our knees and we have been praying like that, but we do not know what to say.'

Themes: Holy Spirit – directing, Missionaries, Parable – Friend at Midnight, Parable – Unjust Judge.

Scriptures: Luke 11:5–13; 18:1–8; Romans 1:8–12; 8:26; 12:12; 1 Corinthians 14:14–16; Ephesians 1:15–19; 3:14–18; 6:13–18; Philippians 4:6; Colossians 1:9–14; 4:2; 1 Thessalonians 1:2; 5:17.

127: Prayer – persistence

A man watched his Uncle Byron fight a bitter battle with cancer. People from the uncle's church were praying and fasting for him around the clock. All over the world friends of the family were asked to pray for him. But as the months, and then a year went by, Byron grew steadily worse.

The nephew only visited his uncle once during his illness. He saw that the slightest movement made him weep with pain. The nephew assumed that would be the last time he would see his uncle. Yet, when I heard this story, a year and a half later, Uncle Byron was completely free of cancer. He wears the scars of battle; his 5' 10" frame is now 10" shorter. His face has new lines drawn by the pain, and walking is severely limited. But his doctors call his recovery a miracle. What would have happened if Uncle Byron had given up when he wasn't healed the first time he prayed – or the tenth, or the 100th?

Themes: Fasting, Parable – Friend at Midnight, Parable – Unjust Judge, Prayer – answered, Prayer – vigil.

Scriptures: Luke 11:5–13; 18:1–8; Romans 1:8–12; 8:26; 12:12; 1 Corinthians 14:14–16; Ephesians 1:15–19; 3:14–18; 6:13–18; Philippians 4:6; Colossians 1:9–14; 4:2; 1 Thessalonians 1:2; 5:17.

128: Prayer – simple

Three hermits lived on an island. Their prayer of intimacy and love was as simple as they were simple: 'We are three; you are three; have mercy on us. Amen.' Miracles sometimes happened when they prayed in this way.

The bishop, however, hearing about the hermits decided that they needed guidance in proper prayer, and so he went to their small island. After instructing the monks, the bishop set sail for the mainland, pleased to have enlightened the souls of such simple men.

Suddenly, off the stern of the ship he saw a huge ball of light skimming across the ocean. It got closer and closer until he could see that it was the three hermits running on top of the water. Once on board the ship they said to the bishop, 'We are so sorry, but we have forgotten some of your teaching. Would you please instruct us again?' The bishop shook his head and replied meekly, 'Forget everything I have taught you and continue to pray in your old way.'

Themes: Bishops, Hunour, Miracles, Monks, Prayer – answered, Simplicity, Walking on water.

Scriptures: 1 Kings 18:30–40; Matthew 6:1–14; Luke 11:1–5; Acts 4:30; Romans 8:26.

129: Prayer – unanswered

Rebecca Templemann was a little girl who went to church. Rebecca – and Megan, her friend from church – caught chicken pox at the same time. Megan recovered very quickly. The church family heard how the Lord had touched the little girl to bring about a speedy recovery, but Rebecca suffered long and hard. There were hundreds of itchy red blisters covering her from scalp to sole. Her dad, Louis Templemann, was the minister of their church family.

One night, when mum was at work as a nurse, Rebecca kept her dad up until 4.30 in the morning, crying and whimpering. He dabbed the raised spots with calamine lotion and tried to encourage her to sleep. Trusting Christ, he prayed for her. But still Rebecca could not sleep.

Eventually Louis began to say to the Lord as he lay on his bed, 'Lord, what is going on? Megan gets a healing. Why not my Rebecca?'

Then he sensed God saying this to him: 'I have given you a greater miracle. You have been given the honour of showing your daughter the nature of a loving father. By your example you have the privilege of teaching her the nature of God. She is learning that she can call out in her agony to her father. Isn't that worth losing a little sleep?'

Themes: Fatherhood, God – Father, Healing, Lord's Prayer, Suffering.

Scriptures: 2 Samuel 11; Psalms 31:9–10; 32; 34:1; 38; 71:6; Hosea 14:2; Matthew 5:12; Mark 3:35; Luke 11:1–4, 13; Romans 5:3–5; 8:15; 14:7–8; 2 Corinthians 5:15; Galatians 2:20; 4:6; 6:9; Ephesians 5:20; Philippians 1:21; 4:12; Hebrews 10:34; 13:15; James 1:2–4; 1 Peter 1:7; 2:5.

130: Promises – not accepted

Last century, around 1830, Crowfoot was born into the Bear Ghost family of Blackfoot Indians. While still a teenager he won distinction for his bravery and scouting ability. He was soon the great chief of the Blackfoot confederacy of Indian nations in southern Alberta, Canada. In 1884, authorities from the Canadian Pacific Railway sought his permission to take the Atlantic to the Pacific railway line through the territory of his people from Medicine Hat to Alberta. In agreeing during the negotiations Canadian Pacific Railway gave Crowfoot, in return, a lifetime rail pass. Crowfoot had a leather case made for the pass. He carried the pass with him, around his neck, wherever he went. However, there is no record of Crowfoot ever using the pass to travel anywhere on Canadian Pacific trains.

Themes: Faith, God – his favour, Grace, Leadership, Salvation – rejected, Trust.

Scriptures: 1 Kings 8:22–53; 2 Chronicles 6:1–42; Romans 1:16–3:20; 3:21–28; 5:2; 10:9; Galatians 2:16; Ephesians 2:1–10.

131: Protection

Friday 7 July 1497, a group of Portuguese sailors spent a night in prayer. The next day they set out on a voyage to circumnavigate the southernmost tip of Africa. Some eighty million tons of water per second sweep down the east coast of Africa and hit the Atlantic head on. It is little wonder the ancient sailors called these dangerous swirling waters, the Cape of Storms.

Vasco da Gama had been sent by the Portuguese king to find the way to India by sea. Da Gama studied the charts and set sail with four ships to round the Cape. On Saturday 18 November the dreaded promontory came into sight. Then, over four days a number of attempts were made to round the Cape. But the wind was dead ahead and they failed. At last, on Wednesday 22 November, at noon, he was successful, having the wind astern. As he rounded the Cape, da Gama looked landward and cried, 'No long will you be called the Cape of Storms – but now *Buono Esperanza* – the Cape of Good Hope.'

Themes: God – his care, Persistence, Prayer, Suffering, Thanksgiving.

Scriptures: Psalms 4; 5; 6; 12; 13; 23; 25; 28; 31; 35; 40:12–17; 44; 54; 59; 61; 62; 64; 69; 70; 77; 89:46–52; 91; 108; 119:153–160, 169–176; 120; 124; 126; 130; 140; 142; 143; 144; Matthew 5:12; Romans 5:2–5; James 1:2–4; 1 Peter 1:6.

132: Ransom

Nigel, a young man who lived in Britain, went on a trip to the United States. He had very little money with him. One day he was driving a borrowed car and went through a stop sign. Of course, the police were there waiting for him! Nigel pleaded with the man in blue, saying that he was a tourist and did not have a lot of money. But the policeman would hear none of his excuses and handed him a ticket. The next day, when Nigel arrived home there was a letter waiting for him. In it was a note from the policeman and a cheque for the amount of the fine.

Themes: Atonement, Cross, Freedom, Jesus – his work, Reconciliation, Redeemed, Rescued.

Scriptures: Exodus 6:6; Psalm 77:14–15; Mark 10:45; Luke 24:21; John 1:29; 8:31–36; 1 Corinthians 1:30; 5:7; 6:19–20; 7:22–23; Galatians 3:13; 4:4–5; 5:1; Ephesians 1:7; 5:2; Titus 2:14; Hebrews 9:15; 1 Peter 1:18–19; 1 John 2:2.

133: Reconciliation

I heard of a tramp in the US who said this.

> I got off at the Pennsylvania depot one day as a tramp, and for a year I begged on the street for a living. One day I touched a man on the shoulder and said, 'Mister, please give me a dime.' As soon as I saw his face I recognised my old father. 'Father, don't you know me?' I asked. Throwing his arms around me he cried, 'I have found you, I have found you. All I have is yours.'

The tramp, who became a Christian, went on to say, 'Men think of it, that I a tramp stood begging my father for ten cents, when for eighteen years he had been looking for me, to give me all he was worth'.

Themes: God – Father, Good Shepherd, Lord's Prayer, Parable – Good Samaritan, Parable – Lost Coin, Parable – Lost Sheep, Parable – Prodigal Son, Salvation.

Scriptures: Isaiah 64:8; Malachi 1:6; 2:10; Luke 10:25–37; 11:1–4; 15:1–7, 8–10, 11–32; 19:10; John 10:1–18; 20:17; Romans 8:17; Galatians 3:26; Hebrews 12:9.

134: Rejection

For those who have been dumped or rejected by someone there are some practical tips.

First, for the women:

1. Go shopping.
2. Eat lots of Haagen-Daz ice cream.
3. Become a nun.
4. Cry a lot until you look like ET.
5. Call him 1,000 times a day and hang up as he answers.

For men who have been dumped or rejected:

1. Do not listen to country music for at least three months.
2. Refer to 'her' not as your 'ex' but as Cruella.
3. Avoid the rebound syndrome except for Elle MacPherson or What's-Her-Name from *Bay Watch*.
4. Return all her gifts COD.
5. Don't slam down the receiver when she rings. Get an airhorn ready by the phone.

Themes: Depression, Divorce, Humour, Love, Marriage, Men, Relationships.

Scriptures: Proverbs 31; Matthew 5:4; Mark 10:2–12; 11:25; Luke 10:27; 1 Corinthians 7:1–16; 13; 2 Corinthians 1:3–7; Ephesians 5:21–33; Philippians 4:8.

135: Relationships

William Inge tells the story of an unhappy quarrelling family in Oklahoma in the early 1920s. The family –

the Rubin Flood family – were all insecure, fearful and continually engulfed in self-pity.

The daughter, Reenie Flood, accepted a blind date to a dance at the country club which was being sponsored by a snobbish socialite family in town. Reenie's date was Sammie Goldenbloom, who was an unwanted orphan. But Sammie was a sensitive boy and a very caring date. Reenie Flood was elated that a person could care for her as did Sammie.

She had danced all evening with Sammie and suddenly realized that no other boy had asked to dance with her. She was concerned that Sammie would think that she was not popular. She decided that she would deceive Sammie into thinking she had been dancing with others. She was actually hiding out with a girlfriend.

While Sammie stood alone, the snobbish socialite sponsor walked over to him and told him how little she thought of him – and of all Jews for that matter. Completely humiliated and dejected, Sammie looked for Reenie. Unable to find her, he left. Later he committed suicide.

Themes: Acceptance, Comfort, Conflict, Courting, Dates, Despair, Families, Persecution, Prejudice, Rejection, Suicide.

Scriptures: 2 Samuel 12; Psalms 6:5–7; 23:4; 46: 55:22; 119:28; Isaiah 25:8; 53:3–4; Hosea 13:14; Matthew 5:4; John 11; Romans 5:1–5; 1 Corinthians 15:54–56; 2 Corinthians 1:3–7; 1 Thessalonians 4:13–18; James 1:2–4; 1 Peter 5:6–7.

136: Relationships

We are living through a period of unprecedented change. Part of that change is the changing status and role of women. The following have been suggested as rules for the new role relationships.

1. The female always makes the rules.
2. The rules are subject to change at any time without prior notification.
3. No male can possibly know all the rules.
4. If the female suspects the males know all the rules, she must immediately change some or all the rules.
5. The female is NEVER wrong.
6. If the female is wrong, it is because of a flagrant misunderstanding which was a direct result of something the male did or said wrong.
7. If the previous rule applies, the male must apologize immediately for causing the misunderstanding.
8. The female can change her mind at any given point in time.
9. The male must never change his mind without written consent from the female.
10. The female has every right to be angry or upset at any time.
11. The male must remain calm at all times, unless the female wants him to be angry or upset.
12. The female must under NO CIRCUMSTANCES let the male know whether or not she wants him to be angry or upset.
13. Any attempt to document these rules could result in bodily harm.
14. If the female has PMT, all rules are null and void.

Themes: Conflict, Family, Man, Marriage, Woman.

Scriptures: Deuteronomy 24:1–5; Proverbs 31; Matthew 5:4, 27–28, 31–32; Mark 10:2–12; 11:25; Luke 10:27; 1 Corinthians 7:1–16; 13; 2 Corinthians 1:3–7; Ephesians 5:21–33; Philippians 4:8.

137: Religion – false

Not long after Kay and Shane were engaged their parents met to discuss arrangements for the wedding. However, Kay's mum Noleen and Shane's dad Terry also fell in love. Noleen and Terry began to meet as often as possible, being consumed with a terrible passion for each other. After the children were married, Terry urged Noleen to leave her husband, but she would not.

Instead, they planned to kill Noleen's husband. Terry gave Paul, a friend, £1,000 to carry out the killing. He agreed to give more money later. On the night of the murder, Terry spent the evening out drinking with the victim. When he arrived home that night, Paul was lying in wait at the top of the stairs. This would have been the sixth attempt to kill Noleen's husband.

As the unsuspecting man reached the top of the stairs he was leaped upon and bludgeoned with a rolling pin. He suffered twenty-nine separate blows to the head. Despite his injuries, he partially undressed and got into bed, where he was later found by the emergency services.

In court, in November 1992, Noleen told the Crown

Court that because of her religious upbringing she would not consider separation or divorce.

Themes: Adultery, Divorce, Ethics, Murder, Selfishness, Sexuality, Sin.

Scriptures: Exodus 20:14; Leviticus 20:10; Deuteronomy 5:18; Proverbs 6:32; Jeremiah 3:8; 5:7; 13:27; Hosea 2:1–5; Matthew 5:7–8; 19:9; Mark 7:21; 10:11, 19; John 8:1–11; 2 Thessalonians 3:6; 2 Timothy 3:5; 2 Peter 2:14.

138: Rescued

Captain Scott F O'Grady was a young man who flies an F-16 jet for the US airforce. On Friday afternoon, 2 June 1995, he was on a flying mission over Banja Luka in Bosnia. Suddenly, a Soviet-made Sam 6 surface-to-air missile blew his plane in half. His cockpit disintegrated in front of him and then there was fire all around him. As he yanked the gold handle of the ejector seat, the explosive bolts hurled off the canopy slightly burning his neck. A few seconds later he pulled the ripcord of his parachute. Floating down he could see what he feared – a truck of Serbian soldiers waiting for him.

When he hit the ground he tore off his chute and made for the trees. He dropped into a bush and put his face in the dirt. He put his green flying gloves over his head and ears. He didn't want his white skin to be seen. He heard men moving about him – only a few feet away – shooting their rifles. They were shouting wildly.

O'Grady did not move for five hours. His thirst was over-powering. At nightfall he was finally able to have a drink from his survival kit. He had a small, simple hand-radio. But he dared not use it. People were so close they would hear his voice or he would easily be traced.

He soon ran out of water. So he prayed for rain and was rewarded with torrential downpours, but he could not find a creek as he crept about at night. Instead he used a sponge to sop up water from dew and squeezed it into his mouth. To stay alive, he ate grass and ants he dug from the ground.

At one point he spent hours lying motionless beneath a cow that was feeding on blades of grass between his legs.

As he moved about at night he began using his hand-held radio, but it was not powerful. Yet, trying to listen to him were NATO jets, spy satellites and radio beacon. Eventually, US intelligence picked up snippets of a garbled message they thought might be O'Grady's. It was enough for airforce officials to tell his father that his boy was out there somewhere.

By now O'Grady was running out of time. His radio batteries would last only seven hours. After nearly a week living on ants and grass he was physically weakening. Now, he was wringing out his woollen socks for drinking water. Although he didn't know it, he was suffering from hypothermia.

The next Thursday night, at eight minutes past midnight, he was huddled in a rocky paddock under a clear sky. He heard three clicks on his radio that made his heart start race. And then, ever so faintly, came the sound he had been longing for, another American air force pilot's voice: 'Basher 52. This is Basher 11 on Alpha. I'm alive and I need help.' Basher 52 was his call number, Basher 11 was his mate TO – Captain Thomas Hanford.

Hanford had been flying for almost an hour searching for his mate. He had three minutes fuel left before he'd have to turn back to base.

'Basher 52 reads you loud and clear', O'Grady was replying to his mate in a hushed cry. But Hanford was wary of traps set by the enemy. So he asked Basher 52 a question to check that it was O'Grady. Eventually Hanford said, 'Copy that! You're alive. Good to hear your voice.' Hanford's voice sounded calm and steady. Actually, he was having trouble flying because he was crying.

Immediately, NATO command was notified that O'Grady had been found. They couldn't be sure how much longer O'Grady could survive. So, NATO command's solution was a surprise dawn raid to rescue Scott.

Dawn was three hours away when marines began scrambling from their racks. From 3.45 am forty aircraft and helicopters began taking to the air. They came from bases in Italy and two aircraft carriers. Some of the planes were designed to jam radio signals. Some planes flew high to direct operations. Some were equipped to knock out ground fire. Then two Sea Stallion assault helicopters were each loaded with forty-one marines.

At 6.35 am — just over an hour after take-off — the gunships spotted yellow smoke from Scott's flare signal. Nine minutes later the two choppers landed. One of them disgorged its forty-one marines to form a ring of safety around the pick-up site. But the chopper that was to pick up Scott landed against a tree stump. Its rear ramp jammed. It had to take off and land again.

Then, dripping wet, waving a pistol, and wearing a green and orange hat to identify himself as 'a stupid American', Scott ran from the trees through the rain, straight to his chopper. He was pulled through a cockpit opening. Scott mouthed the words, 'Thank you'. But he wasn't safe yet. As the pilots skimmed the ground at thirty metres, enemy bullets winked off the blades. By 7.30 am the Sea Stallion chopper was landing on the deck of the *USS Kearsarge* an amphibious assault craft in the Adriatic.

Scott O'Grady had been successfully rescued. One of President Clinton's national security advisers announced the incredible news that the young airforce captain had been found and rescued by the marines in a daring raid after six days behind enemy lines. Mr Clinton hailed the rescue saying, 'All Americans rejoice with me at the successful rescue of Captain Scott O'Grady tonight and join his parents in their relief after days of uncertainty and anguish.'

To bring out that one lost airman – in all – $6 billion worth of equipment and the attention of US and NATO high command were brought into operation.

Themes: God – Father, God – his love, Good Shepherd, Lord's Prayer, Parable – Good Samaritan, Parable – Lost Coin, Parable – Lost Sheep, Parable – Prodigal Son, People – value of, Salvation, Testimony.

Scriptures: Isaiah 64:8; Malachi 1:6; 2:10; Luke 10:25–37; 11:1–4; 15:1–7, 8–10, 11–32; 19:10; John 10:1–18; 20:17; Romans 8:17, 31–39; Galatians 3:26; Hebrews 12:9.

139: Rescued

Gregory Robertson was a parachute safety and training adviser. He was also a veteran of some 1,500 parachute jumps. One day he followed six other sky divers out of a plane 3.22 kilometres above the ground.

When, at 2.75 kilometres the six attempted to link

hands, Debbie Williams accidentally collided with one of the skydivers and knocked herself unconscious. Seeing her plight, Robertson tucked his arms to his sides and using his shoulders to steer himself, went after Debbie. Plunging downward at 322 kilometres per hour, he was able to catch her. Manoeuvring her into a sitting position, Robertson yanked her ripcord. They were at 823 metres! At 609.5 metres he opened his own chute. Ten seconds later he would have slammed into the ground.

Themes: God – Father, God – his love, Good Shepherd, Lord's Prayer, Parable – Good Samaritan, Parable – Lost Coin, Parable – Lost Sheep, Parable – Prodigal Son, People – value of, Salvation.

Scriptures: Isaiah 64:8; Malachi 1:6; 2:10; Luke 10:25–37; 11:1–4; 15:1–7, 8–10, 11–32; 19:10; John 10:1–18; 20:17; Romans 8:17, 31–39; Galatians 3:26; Hebrews 12:9.

140: Resurrection

A vase was found closely sealed in a mummy pit in Egypt by the English traveller Wilkinson who sent it to the British Museum. The librarian had the misfortune to drop it and it was broken. From the ruins he gathered a few peas, old, wrinkled and as hard as stones. The peas were planted carefully under a glass on 4 June 1844. At the end of thirty days they had sprouted and were growing nicely. They had been buried as dead, perhaps for 3,000 years, and yet were brought to life by the librarian.

Themes: Death, Defeat, Good news.

Scriptures: Mark 1:1; 16:1–8; Luke 24:1–12; John 20:1–31; Romans 1:3–4; 1 Corinthians 15; 2 Corinthians 13:4; Ephesians 1:19–20.

141: Reunion

During the Second World War, seventeen-year-old Leon Frost was on the run from the KGB. At one point he sneaked home and knocked on the door. A voice the other side said, 'Who is it?'

'It's your son – Leon,' he said. 'Open up . . .' In a second the door was open and mother and son were in each other's arms. Then Leon turned to his dad and his thirteen-year-old sister Irena. He told them he had come home to say goodbye. All Leon took with him was a photo of his brother. Leon made his way to Warsaw where he was arrested and sent to prison.

At the end of the war there was no way of finding his family. He emigrated to Adelaide and started work at Norwood Engineering. Eventually he married Doris in the Birkenhead Methodist Church.

Leon began trying to track down his family. One day a letter came from the Red Cross. It told of his brother's death during the war. Leon read it without saying anything. The years went by but still he was unable to find his family.

One day Leon's daughter Patti wrote to a newspaper in

Poland. A fortnight later a letter arrived. Her eyes widened as she read the contents. She pushed the letter into her dad's hands. It read, 'Your parents died in Siberia during the war, but your sister Irena may still be alive, living in England.' It was signed by a cousin. Patti wrote another letter this time to the Red Cross in England. Just weeks later a letter came back. Leon's son Terry rang him. 'Sit down Dad,' he said, 'I've got great news.' Speechless, Leon listened. Irena was alive. She was married with a child and was living in Los Angeles. The Red Cross in England had sent a letter to Irena in Los Angeles. Irena then began phoning every Frost in Australia. Eventually she got Leon's son Terry. Terry gave her his father's number. Leon took a deep breath and dialled. A woman's voice answered. 'Irena?' asked Leon. 'Yes,' said the woman. Tears streamed down Leon's face. He had found his sister. 'My sister,' he said in Polish, 'I thought you were dead.'

Two months later Irena flew to Australia. At the Mt Gambier aerodrome in South Australia, seventy-two-year-old Leon was waiting. They embraced each other. 'This is the happiest day of my life,' Leon said. Leon has since visited Irena in California. 'I feel so grateful I've had the chance to get to know her again,' he said. 'I spent so many years believing she was dead. Now I feel a peace I've only ever dreamed of.

Themes: Good Shepherd, Parable – Good Samaritan, Parable – Lost Coin, Parable – Lost Sheep, Parable – Prodigal Son, Reconciliation, Salvation.

Scriptures: Isaiah 64:8; Malachi 1:6; 2:10; Luke 10:25–37; 15:1–7, 8–10, 11–32; 19:10; John 10:1–18; 20:17; Romans 8:17; Galatians 3:26; Hebrews 12:9.

142: Reunion

Louis Pasteur (1822–95) was a French microbiologist who discovered vaccines for cholera and rabies. Pasteur and his wife had five children, but three of them died as young children, two in the same year as Pasteur's father died. 'They die, one after another, our poor children. You see what a fragile thing it is, this life of ours,' he said bitterly. The Pasteurs were left with a son, Jean-Baptiste, and a daughter Marie-Louise – or 'Zizi', as they called her.

Then, in 1870 Pasteur's work was interrupted by the devastating Franco-Prussian war. His son, Jean-Baptiste, had gone to war, but he had not been heard of for some time. In January 1871 a near starving Paris surrendered. The defeated French troops straggled back in retreat, begging for bread along the way, their uniforms in tatters. Even though they had not heard from Jean-Baptiste for some time the Pasteurs were convinced they could find their son. Pasteur's old friend and neighbour, Jules Vercel, saw him start out, accompanied by his wife and daughter, on Tuesday 24 January, in a half broken-down old carriage.

On the Friday they reached Pontarlier by roads made almost impracticable by the snow, the carriage now a mere wreck. The town was full of soldiers, some crouching round fires in the street, others stepping across their dead horses and begging for a little straw to lie on. Many had taken refuge in the church and were lying on the steps of the altar; a few were attempting to bandage their frozen feet, threatened with gangrene.

Mme Pasteur asked anxiously after her son. 'All that I can tell you,' a soldier said, 'is that out of the 1,200 men of that battalion there are but 300 left.' As she was questioning another, a soldier who was passing stopped; 'Sergeant Pasteur? Yes, he is alive; I slept by him last night at Chaffois. He has remained behind; he is ill. You might meet him on the road towards Chaffois.'

The Pasteurs had barely passed the Pontarlier gate when a rough cart came by. A soldier muffled in his great coat, his hand resting on the edge of the cart, started with surprise. He hurried down. The family embraced without a word, so great was their emotion.

> **Themes:** God – Father, Good Shepherd, Lord's Prayer, Parable – Good Samaritan, Parable – Lost Coin, Parable – Lost Sheep, Parable – Prodigal Son, Salvation.
>
> **Scriptures:** Isaiah 64:8; Malachi 1:6; 2:10; Luke 10:25–37; 11:1–4; 15:1–7, 8–10, 11–32; 19:10; John 10:1–18; 20:17; Romans 8:17; Galatians 3:26; Hebrews 12:9.

143: Revenge

A woman went to Ibn Saud, the first king of Saudi Arabia. She requested that the man who killed her husband be put to death. The man had fallen from the top of a palm tree when he had been gathering dates and landed on this lady's husband and killed him.

The king said, 'It is your right to exact compensation, and it is also your right to ask for this man's life. But it is my right to decree how he shall die. You shall take this man with you and he shall be tied to the foot of a palm tree and then you shall climb to the top of the tree and cast yourself down upon him from that height. In that way you will take his life as he took your husband's. Or perhaps,' Ibn Saud added, 'you would prefer after all to take the blood money?' The widow took the money.

Themes: Avenger, Humour, Justice, Mercy, Solomon, Vengeance, Wisdom.

Scriptures: Genesis 4:10–16, 23–24; 9:5–6; Leviticus 19:18; Numbers 35:9–15, 16–21, 22–28; Joshua 10:13; Judges 12:3–6; 1 Kings 3:16–28; 2 Kings 9:7; Psalm 94; Matthew 5:38–42; Romans 12:17–19; 13:4; 1 Thessalonians 4:6; Revelation 6:10; 19:2.

144: Revival

On 1 July 1857 a quiet but keen Christian businessman named Jeremiah Lanphier took up an appointment as a city missionary in down-town New York. The church was suffering from a depletion of membership as people moved out to better homes. Lanphier decided to invite others to join him in a Wednesday noon prayer-meeting. On the first Wednesday he waited for half an hour before one person came. Six in all came the first day. Twenty came the second Wednesday. Within six months 10,000 businessmen were gathering daily in New York for prayer, and a revival in America had begun.

Within two years, two million converts had been added to the American churches.

Themes: Church growth, Conversion, Intercession, Prayer, Prayer – answered, Prayer – constant, Prayer – vigil.

Scriptures: Acts 4:30–31; Romans 1:8–12; 12:12; 1 Corinthians 14:14–16; Ephesians 1:15–19; 3:14–18; 6:13–18; Philippians 4:6; Colossians 1:9–14; 4:2; 1 Thessalonians 1:2; 5:17.

145: Rivalry

There's no doubt that the *National Geographic* magazine has some incredible stories and pictures in it. In one issue there was a picture of a fossil. It was a fossil of two sabre-toothed cats locked in combat. One of the cats had attacked and bitten deep into the leg of the other. The massive tooth of one was stuck firmly in the body of the other. Of course, neither could feed nor live normally. Because of that vicious attack, they were both destined to die.

Themes: Death, Division, Divorce, Enemies, Fighting, Fruit of the Spirit, Jealousy, Love – of enemies, Marriage, Paul – opponents, Peace, Spirit – fruit of.

Scriptures: Psalms 4:8; 55:18; Isaiah 26:3; Matthew 5:9; Luke 6:27–30; Romans 8:6; 10:15; 12:18, 20; 14:17, 19; 15:13; 1 Corinthians 1:10–17; 7:15; 13; 2 Corinthians 13:11;

Galatians 5:19–22; Colossians 3:12–17; 1 Thessalonians 5:13; 2 Thessalonians 3:16; 2 Timothy 2:22; Hebrews 12:14; 1 Peter 3:11.

146: Substitution

A baby was born at Christmas time in New York. The birth went well, but then complications set in. The specialist approached the anxious father who had been waiting all afternoon outside the intensive care ward. The doctor, gowned in white, said to the father, 'I am sorry to have to tell you that your baby lived only two hours. We did everything we could to save it but in the end nothing could be done.'

The father had known that something was wrong and had prepared to say something in particular to the doctor if things turned out the way they did. The father said 'I read recently that human eyes are needed for corneal operations. Could our baby's eyes be used to enable someone to see again?' They could. The next day the Red Cross carried an eye each to two different hospitals. In one hospital, a corneal graft restored the sight of a working man with a large family. In the other hospital, sight was given to a mother.

Themes: Gifts, Gratitude, Love – of others, Substitution, Suffering.

Scriptures: Exodus 6:6; Psalm 77:14–15; Mark 10:45; Luke 10:27; 24:21; John 1:29; 15:12–17; 1 Corinthians 1:30; 5:7; 6:19–20; 7:22–23; 13; Galatians 3:13; 4:4–5; 5:1; Ephesians 1:7; 5:2; Titus 2:14; Hebrews 9:15; 1 Peter 1:18–19; 1 John 2:2.

147: Sacrifice

C T Studd was brought up in nineteenth century luxury. His father was retired in Leicestershire spending the fortune made as a tea planter in North India. C T became captain of the Cambridge University XI and in 1882 he was in Australia recovering the Ashes.

All of this changed, for he became a Christian through his father and sensed God's call to the mission field. So, in his early 20's he was in Shanghai as a missionary. A few years later he was married.

Here is his description of their first home. 'The first house we had was a haunted house . . . It was just bare white-washed walls, and brick floors, but very unevenly bricked, with a fireplace in the centre, and brick bed. Our mattress was a cotton-wool quilt about an inch thick. That was our bed for the first three years, until it became so infested with scorpions that we had to have it pulled down. Then we had a wooden sort of planking.

'For five years we never went outside our doors without a volley of curses from our neighbours.'

Themes: Contentment, Conversion, Hatred, Joy, Materialism, Missionaries, Persecution, Perseverance, Suffering.

Scriptures: John 10:28–30; Acts 9:1–22; 2 Corinthians 1:8–11; 4:1–18; Philippians 4:11; 1 Timothy 6:6–8; Hebrews 13:5; 1 Peter 1:3–9.

148: Saved

Normally the flight from Nassau to Miami took Walter Wyatt, Jr, only sixty-five minutes. But on 5 December 1986, he attempted it after thieves had looted the navigational equipment in his Beechcraft. With only a compass and a hand-held radio, Walter flew into skies blackened by storm clouds.

When his compass began to girate, Walter concluded he was headed in the wrong direction. He flew his plane below the clouds, hoping to spot something, but soon he knew he was lost. He put out a Mayday call, alerting a Coast Guard Falcon search plane which intended to lead him to an emergency landing strip only six miles away.

Suddenly Wyatt's right engine coughed its last and died. The fuel tank had run dry. Around 8 pm Wyatt could do little more than glide the plane into the water. He survived the crash, but his plane disappeared quickly, leaving him bobbing on the water in a leaky life vest.

With blood on his forehead, Wyatt floated on his back. Suddenly he felt a hard bump against his body. A shark had found him. Wyatt kicked the intruder and wondered if he would survive the night. He managed to stay afloat for the next ten hours.

In the morning, there was still no sign of an aeroplane,

but in the water a dorsal fin was headed for him. Twisting, he felt the hide of a shark brush against him, and in a moment, two more bull sharks sliced through the water towards him. Again he kicked out, and they veered away, but he was nearing exhaustion.

Then he heard the hum of a distant aircraft. When it was within half a mile, he waved his orange vest. The pilot dropped a smoke canaster and radioed the cutter *Cape York*, which was twelve minutes away: 'Get moving, cutter! There's a shark targeting this guy!'

As the *Cape York* pulled alongside Wyatt, a Jacob's ladder was dropped over the side. Wyatt climbed wearily out of the water and on to the ship, where he fell to his knees and kissed the deck.

Themes: Atonement, Christmas, Easter, Evangelism, God – his love, Rescued, Salvation.

Scriptures: Isaiah 64:8; Malachi 1:6; 2:10; Luke 11:1–4; 15:1–7, 8–10, 11–32; 10:25–37; 19:10; John 10:1–18; 20:17; Romans 8:17, 31–39; Galatians 3:26; Hebrews 12:9.

149: Saved

Franz-Josef I of Austria was the last emperor of the Habsburg empire which had its origins in the thirteenth century. Franz-Josef died on 21 November 1916, during the First World War. A few days later, at the funeral on 30 November, the splendrous pageantry of one of the greatest empires Europe had ever known was displayed for the last time. Eight black horses drew the hearse containing the coffin which was draped in the black and gold imperial colours. The hearse was preceded by carriages filled with wreaths. In turn these carriages were preceded by barouches seating the highest court dignitaries. Behind this procession came the carriages carrying the members of the family and the foreign officials. Mounted guards in their dress uniform escorted the procession along the Ringstrasse, across Vienna, to St Stephen's Cathedral. A band played sombre music.

After the service the cortège covered the few hundred metres to the Capuchin crypt on foot. By the light of flaming torches, the cortège descended the steps of the crypt. At the bottom was a great iron door leading to the Habsburg family crypt. Behind the door was the abbot. With the Grand Master of the court he began the ritual dialogue, established centuries before.

The Grand Master, Prince Montenuovo, cried out, 'Open!' The abbot responded, 'Who are you? Who asks to enter here?' The Grand Master began to list the emperor's thirty-seven titles, 'We bear the remains of his Imperial and Apostolic Majesty, Franz-Josef I, by the grace of God Emperor of Austria, King of Hungary, Defender of the Faith, Prince of Bohemiah-Moravia, Grand Duke of Lombardy, Venezia, Styrgia . . .' And so he continued through the whole thirty-seven titles. However, the abbot called back, 'We know him not. Who goes there?' The Prince spoke again. This time he used a much abbreviated and less ostentatious title reserved for times of expediency. But, again, the abbot responded, 'We know him not. Who goes there?'

The Grand Master tried a third time. He stripped the emperor of all but the humblest of titles. Going down on his knees, he simply cried out, 'We bear the body of Franz-Josef, our brother, a sinner like us all.'

At that the door swung open and the abbot said, 'Enter then.' And Franz-Josef was admitted.

Themes: Access, Acceptance, Grace, Heaven, Humility, Salvation, Works.

Scriptures: Romans 3:19–31; 5:1–2; Galatians 2:16; Ephesians 2:8–9; 2 Timothy 1:9.

150: Second coming

A few years ago the influential American magazine *Harper's* hired some advertising consultants to organize a strategy for the return of Jesus. The consultants suggested that he arrive at 7 am in New York. He ought to arrive by a small airline company. That would be a sign of humility. In the first news conference he was to strike the tone 'it's good to be back'. Then he should board the glass-domed vehicle called 'Donkey One'. On the second day he should have an outdoor press conference. This would give easy miracle opportunities. Rain wouldn't impress so the consultants suggested hail.

Themes: Advent, Christmas, Eschatology, Humour, Miracles.

Scriptures: Matthew 1:18–2:23; Luke 1:5–2:40; 1 Corinthians 5:5; 1 Thessalonians 4:13–5:11; 2 Thessalonians 2:1–12; Hebrews 9:28; 2 Peter 3:1–18.

151: Self esteem

Margaret's parents did not really love her. In fact, they wanted a boy. Margaret's father gave her very little time. As a small girl she would look up to him, but he did not seem to notice her. At other times, when he was in a bad mood, he would push her out of the way.

As she grew up, she used bad language as a way of getting her parents' attention. She told her parents that she hated them. They yelled back that they hated her also. More than once she ran away from home. But, she had to come home because she ran out of money. Margaret loved sport and was good at it, but her parents said that she was wasting her time. She ought to be studying. She could never get high enough marks to please her parents.

The years went by and then, at last, marriage came. She thought that marriage would sort out her life. But marriage only seemed to make things worse. Once the shine had gone out of her marriage, it was hell! There were times when Margaret was belted by her husband for over-running the tight family budget, or for making mistakes. Their friends noticed and sympathised. Margaret felt even more sorry for herself and her appearance suffered as her self-esteem dropped. She thought she was going mad.

Interestingly, Margaret is a Christian. With her mind, she accepted that God loved her so much that he gave his only Son for her. But, in her heart, she felt that God was remote and had a revulsion of her. Life was a treadmill, there was no joy in it, only painful endurance. Her conclusion was, 'I wish I was dead'. But then she felt guilty that she had displeased God. If only she could please someone, but she felt she could not.

Themes: Bad language, Commitment, Conflict, Domestic violence, Families, Marriage, Parenting.

Scriptures: Deuteronomy 24:1–5; Matthew 5:27–29, 31–32; 19:3–12; Mark 10:2–12; Luke 10:27; John 14:15–24; Acts 5:29; 1 Corinthians 7:1–11; 13.

152: Self image

When David Burns was a student, he kept a journal. It was filled with private memories. Some were painful recollections from childhood – times when he felt hurt, confused, lonely and insecure. He described fragments of dreams and intensely personal feelings of anger and hatred, as well as things he enjoyed such as magic stores and coin shops. Then a terrible thing happened. After dinner one night he realized that he had left his journal in a cloakroom outside the dining hall. Terrified that somebody might read it and find out the truth about him, he raced back. It was gone. Weeks passed and eventually he gave up all hope of finding it. A month later, he was hanging up his coat in the same place. He saw his brown tattered journal, just where he had left it. Nervously he picked it up and leafed through these private pages. He found a stranger had written this entry: 'God bless you. I am a lot like you, only I don't keep a diary, and I'm grateful to know there are others like me. I hope things turn out well for you.' Tears came to David's eyes.

It had never dawned on him that anyone could have the same worries and inner fears, yet still care about him.

Themes: Anxiety, Fear, Healing – inner, Inner healing, Weakness, Worry.

Scriptures: Psalms 55:22; 118:6; Luke 12:22–34; 1 Corinthians 10; 13; 2 Corinthians 12:1–13; Philippians 4:6; Hebrews 13:5; 1 Peter 5:7.

153: Service

Marion Preminger was born in Hungary in 1913. She was raised in a castle with an aristocratic and wealthy family, surrounded with maids, tutors, governesses, butlers, and chauffeurs.

She attended school in Vienna. At a Viennese ball, she met a handsome young man, the son of a Viennese doctor. They fell in love and when she was eighteen years old, they eloped – but the marriage lasted only one year.

Marion returned to Vienna to begin a life as an actress. While she was auditioning for a play, she met the young German director, Otto Preminger. They fell in love and soon married. When Preminger went to America to begin a career as a movie director, she went with him. After a while, caught up in the superficial excitement of Hollywood, Marion began to live the sordid life that some people live in Hollywood. Preminger divorced her.

She returned to Europe, living the life of a Paris socialite until 1948. Then she read that Dr Albert Schweitzer was making one of his periodic visits to Europe, so she phoned his secretary and made an appointment for the next day.

She found Schweitzer playing the village church organ. He invited her to dine at his house. After dinner, Marion knew she had found what she had been looking for. She was with Schweitzer every day during his visit, and when he returned to Africa, he invited her to come to Lamberene and work in his hospital. That was her calling.

There the girl who was raised like a princess became a servant . . . and changed bandages, bathed bodies, and fed lepers. There she became free.

Themes: Calling, Divorce, Humility, Leadership, Life – purpose, Marriage, Materialism, Money, Purpose.

Scriptures: Deuteronomy 24:1–5; Matthew 5:27–29, 31–32; 19:3–12; Mark 10:2–12; Luke 10:27; John 14:15–24; Acts 5:29; 1 Corinthians 7:1–11; 13; 2 Corinthians 4:1–18; 11:16–23; Philippians 2:1–11.

154: Sex

Michael was a member of a church youth group. Michael was seventeen, doing his final year at high school. Sometimes he drove his dad's car. One night the group went ten-pin bowling. Vicki was on the same bowling team. She went to the same school as Michael and had been at youth group for quite a few weeks, but they had never taken much notice of each other until this particular night. Things moved pretty fast between them and Michael organized it so that no one went back to the church with him except Vicki. They took the long way back to the church and stopped in a poorly lit street near a creek. Neither of them planned it but they had sex in the car. They both felt guilty and that they had blown it badly. They talked about it and agreed not to have sex again. For a while they felt nervous with people, wondering if anyone could tell that they had done it. But, all seemed well and they started going out regularly. A few weeks after the ten-pin bowling night Vicki came up to Michael at school. She was crying. She had discovered that she was pregnant. Michael was stunned and went hot and cold all at once. Vicki said that she could not tell her parents as they would be devastated and might throw her out of home. She thought she would get an abortion.

Themes: Abortion, Anxiety, Courting, Dating, Fornication, Worry.

Scriptures: Exodus 20:13–14; Job 31:15; Psalms 22:9–10; 55:22; 71:6; 118:6; 139; Ecclesiastes 11:5; Isaiah 49:1, 5; Jeremiah 1:5; Luke 12:22–34; Romans 1:26–27; 1 Corinthians 6:13; 10; 13; 2 Corinthians 12:1–13; Ephesians 5:3; Philippians 4:6; 1 Thessalonians 4:3; Hebrews 13:5; 1 Peter 5:7.

155: Sex

A couple went for their annual check up. The doctor saw the man first and asked him how he had been feeling. 'I have one problem, Doc. The first time my wife and I make love, everything is fine, but the second time I sweat a lot'. The doctor completed the physical and then examined the wife.

'Your husband says the first time you make love is perfect, but that he perspires the second time. Do you know why?'

'Of course I do!' she replied. 'The first time is in winter and the second time is in the summer.'

Themes: Humour, Marriage.

Scriptures: 1 Corinthians 7:1–16; 1 Timothy 4:1–5.

156: Sex

Stephanie Marrian, forty-five, former model and actress tells her story.

I finally split up with my last partner after twelve months when I found out that he was living with another woman. He was the biggest creep in the world. We parted in 1990, but it took me until the end of last year to get over the shock.

I felt he'd made a fool of me and I couldn't stand the thought of what the next man might do. The last time we had sex was on his birthday – 24 August 1990 – and it wasn't anything to write home about.

Then last year, I became a Christian. That means I believe sex outside marriage is wrong, so unless I change my views or marry, I'll never have sex again.

I've been celibate before. I was for four-and-a-half years in my mid-20s. I was a topless model at the time, and I couldn't bear the way men assumed that if you went out with them, you would end up in bed. It was the late 70s and it seemed everybody was doing it, but I had old-fashioned ideas and never got into a casual relationship. I was waiting for Mr Right.

I was twenty-nine when he found me. Before that, the earth never moved for me during sex, but it did with him. Then I ruined it all by having a brief affair. I hoped I could win him back, and so I was celibate for six years, but he married someone else.

I don't miss sex. I guess I have learned to live without it. But I'm caught in a trap. I don't see any point in getting married unless you intend to have children, and at forty-five, that's not very likely. So it's quite possible that I'll never have sex again, which is quite a daunting prospect.

Cliff Richards would be my ideal man, so if he ever reads this, perhaps he could contact me.

Themes: Celibacy, Conversion, Divorce, Faithfulness, Fornication, Men, Relationships.

Scriptures: Deuteronomy 24:1–5; Matthew 5:27–29, 31–32; 19:3–12; Mark 10:2–13; Luke 10:27; John 14:15–24; Acts 5:29; 1 Corinthians 7:1–11; 13.

157: Sexism

An Oxford professor chose to ignore the fact that women were part of the university. He would always begin his lectures, 'Gentlemen'. Even when there were forty women and ten men he would stubbornly address them as 'Gentlemen'. Once he was faced with forty-six women and one lone man. He gritted his teeth, sighed and began his lecture, 'Sir'.

Themes: Humour, Men, Women.

Scriptures: Proverbs 31; Ephesians 5:21–33; Colossians 3:18–4:1.

158: Sexual abuse

A woman nervously told of her father repeatedly molesting her as a young girl. She sought help to try to thaw out a frozen response to her husband's sexual advances. She said, 'I'm not sure if I can ever really give myself to my husband sexually. I know I should . . . I've tried. And my husband has been wonderfully patient. But nothing helps. It's been six years! I don't see how I can ever feel good about sex. The effects of my dad's sin are just too deep.'

Themes: Damaged emotions, Domestic violence, Fathers, Healing – inner, Inner-healing, Marriage, Parenting.

Scriptures: Mark 2:1–12; Romans 12:10; Ephesians 6:1–4; Colossians 3:18–21.

159: Sexuality

Ryan was twenty-nine and single. He went on a Christian camp where, one night, the speaker gave a meaningful and powerful plea for sexual purity. Just before going to bed a small group of campers gathered for devotions. Ryan had been particularly agitated by the talk that evening. So he used this time for confession and prayer. The group sat in stark silence. He told the members about his sexual desires and his attempts to handle them. He was guilty of neither adultery nor fornication. But he went on, tearfully, to tell his friends that he did make use of pornography and masturbation to meet his sexual needs. When Ryan had finished pouring out his sexual troubles, he asked the group to pray. Specifically he asked them to pray that the Lord would take away his sexual hungers so that he could not be tempted again. At that point one of the group interrupted his pleas and Ryan was rightly told that the sexual drive was a gift from God, and that it was not to be taken away but properly handled with God's power.

Themes: Forgiveness, Fruit of the Spirit, Guilt, Lust, Masturbation, Pornography, Spirit – fruit of.

Scriptures: Matthew 5:27–30; Romans 7:1–23; 1 Corinthians 7:8–9; Galatians 5:16–17; Ephesians 2:3; 4:22; Colossians 3:5; 2 Timothy 2:22; Titus 2:11–13; 1 Peter 2:11; 4:3; 1 John 2:15–16.

160: Sin

Tom Rathman was hunting deer in the Tehema Wildlife Area near Red Bluff in northern California. As he lifted his head to look over the ledge above, he felt a rattlesnake striking at him, just missing his right ear.

The snake's fangs got snagged in the neck of his turtle-neck sweater. Then the snake coiled around his neck. He grabbed the snake behind the head and could feel the warm venom running down the skin of his neck.

Falling backwards down the steep slope he ended up wedged between some rocks. The snake struck again. Eight times it attacked him, hitting him with its nose below his eyes about four times. Its fangs were like darning needles. The man finally was able to choke the snake to death, but he could barely shake the dead snake off his hand: 'I had to prise my fingers from its neck,' he said.

Themes: Fear, Habits, Old life, Past.

Scriptures: Mark 10:50; Ephesians 4:25–32; 5:3–14; Colossians 3:5–11; Hebrews 12:1.

161: Sin – disclosed

Last century, the British warship *Sparrow* was pursuing the *Nancy*, a Spanish ship suspected of piracy. When the British boarded the *Nancy* not a shred of incriminating evidence could be found. Nevertheless, the ship was escorted to the port of Kingston in Jamaica.

While this was going on another British ship, the *Abergavenny*, was cruising through the same area. One day, off the coast of Haiti, the officer in charge noticed a dead bullock in the water which was surrounded by sharks. He ordered the bullock to be towed behind the ship so they could catch one of the sharks. It turned out to be an unusually large shark.

When they opened it up, they found in the stomach of the big fish a parcel of papers, tied around with string. The papers had to do with a ship called the *Nancy*. The papers were kept in case they might be useful. They were handed in at the port of Kingston. At this same time, the captain and crew of the *Nancy* were becoming excited about the prospect of being released. But then they were confronted with the papers from the shark: the papers are now in the Institute Museum of Jamaica.

Themes: Confession, God – omniscient, Guilt. Hiding.

Scriptures: Numbers 32:23; Job 26:6; 31:4; Psalms 17:3; 33:13–15; 139; Proverbs 15:11; Jeremiah 12:3; 23:24; Amos 9:2–4; Jonah 1:3; Mark 2:1–12; John 2:24; Hebrews 4:13; 1 John 1:8–9.

162: Spiritual warfare

An African who had recently become a Christian was explaining to a friend what it was like to be a Christian. He said, 'It is as if there were two dogs inside of me. One of the dogs is white and the other is black. And they are always fighting.'

'Which one wins?' asked the friend.

'It depends which one I feed,' he replied.

Themes: Enemies, Evil, Good, Life, New life, Old life, Spiritual battle.

Scriptures: Psalm 1; Romans 6:1–14; 7:14–23; 8:31–39; 1 Corinthians 4:16; 9:24–27; 16:13; 2 Corinthians 10:1–6; Galatians 5:16–26; Ephesians 3:16–17; 4:17–5:2; 6:10–20; Colossians 3:1–17; 1 Timothy 1:18.

163: Spiritual warfare

Tom Walker tells a story from his childhood.

> I used to stay at my uncle's farm in Sussex during the long weeks of summer ... My favourite bovine companion was Bill the bull. He was a huge brown and white Herefordshire bull with splendid horizontal horns and a shining ring in his nose. I reckoned that we had a good relationship going and that he was genuinely my friend. Certainly, tethered up in his stall he only grunted kindly at me, and never showed a moment's violence or antagonism. 'Watch him,' the cowhand

would say, 'you never know with a bull. Never trust him out in the field, and never get in a corner with him in the cowshed. He'll go for yer.'

I remembered that advice when I was sauntering through the field at the back of the farm. The cows were grazing peacefully, and some distance away I could see Bill eyeing me as I passed through the herd. Whether my red shirt caught his eye, or whether he was in a bad mood that morning I do not know, but suddenly he was trotting menacingly towards me. I walked faster, but did not want to give him any impression of fright or panic. Soon his head was down and he was coming for me at full gallop. I headed for the nearest gate as hard as I could but within seconds it was obvious that I had no chance of getting to the gate before he had me on his horns. As I ran I saw a stick on the ground, or rather, it was more of a reed than a stick. It was certainly not an adequate weapon against Bill in full flight. But remembering all the advice I had ever heard about man's mastery over animals, I picked the reed up and stood my ground, staring him firmly in the eye. Snorting hard, Bill stopped and stared back at me. Threatening him fiercely with the bent reed, I drew myself up to my full height of 4 ft 9 in, and as Bill turned his head away, I then backed slowly to the gate. It was an adventure and a half for a nine year old but it taught a lesson of immense significance in spiritual warfare. If you cannot win by brute strength or by hasty retreat, stand your ground. Your weapons may seem inadequate, but because they are God-given they enable you to win in the warfare against Satan.

Themes: Enemies, Evil, Good, Life, New life, Old life, Spiritual battle.

Scriptures: Psalm 1; Romans 6:1–14; 7:14–23; 8:31–39; 1 Corinthians 4:16; 9:24–27; 16:13; 2 Corinthians 10:1–6; Galatians 5:16–26; Ephesians 3:16–17; 4:17–5:2; 6:10–20; Colossians 3:1–17; 1 Timothy 1:18.

164: Spiritual warfare

Carlos Annacondia conducts Christian missions in South America. Some of them are out in the open in a natural amphitheatre. A large stage is erected, and behind that a very large marquee is erected. The crowds gather.

There are usually tens of thousands of people there. So much has the Spirit of God overshadowed the work of Carlos Annacondia that ropes are put up around the platform to stop people coming forward to submit their lives to Jesus.

Towards the end of the talk Carlos has to ask people to stay where they are until the end of his appeal. At the end of the appeal for people to receive Christ the ropes are lowered and there is a rushing and surge of many hundreds of people seeking the forgiveness of Christ in their lives. They are prayed for and encouraged to go on in their new life in Christ.

Then Annacondia explains that he is going to ask the Holy Spirit to come to release those who are under Satan's bondage. He tells them people will fall down. They are not to touch them. His helpers will deal with them. Then Carlos prays. Again, scores of people right across the crowd fall down as dead or screaming. Then, out from the large marquee come the stretcher bearers. They pick up those who have fallen down and take them back to what is known as the 'intensive care unit'. There they minister to these folk. Sometimes for six hours they pray, commanding the spirits to leave in the name of Jesus. There is much rejoicing as spirits leave people and they experience the new freedom in Christ.

But, all is not plain sailing. As well as the eager crowd, there are Satanists who will often set up a booth up at the very back. Witches will attempt to cast spells or hexes on the meeting. When those on the stage sense Satan's attacks and the curses, they stamp their feet on the floor of the stage. For underneath there's a group committed to praying continually for the meeting and that God will change lives.

Themes: Enemies, Evil, Exorcism, Good, Life, Mission, New life, Old life, Prayer, Revival, Satanists, Spiritual battle.

Scriptures: Psalm 1; Mark 1:21–28; 5:1–20; 7:24–30; 9:14–29; Romans 6:1–14; 7:14–23; 8:31–39; 1 Corinithians 4:16; 9:24–27; 16:13; 2 Corinithians 10:1–6; Galatians 5:16–26; Ephesians 3:16–17; 4:17–5:2; 6:10–20; Colossians 3:1–17; 1 Timothy 1:18.

165: *Spiritual warfare*

James Fraser worked among the Lisu people in China. They worshipped demons. He would lead a family to the Lord. The next day one would be sick, and in a few days one would die, and they would go back to demon worship. James became so frustrated. Nevertheless God told him to pray for hundreds of Lisu families to be converted. He urged his prayer group at home to pray, and he entered into spiritual warfare – claiming these people for Christ.

Finally, one day, when he was at his wits end, God suddenly said to him, 'The strong man is bound.'

Soon whole communities of Lisu people began turning to Christ – even some James had never been to.

Themes: Enemies, Evil, Good, Life, New life, Old life, Prayer, Spiritual battle, Strong Man.

Scriptures: Psalm 1; Mark 3:20–27; Romans 6:1–14; 7:14–23; 8:31–39; 1 Corinthians 4:16; 9:24–27; 16:13; 2 Corinthians 10:1–6; Galatians 5:16–26; Ephesians 3:16–17; 4:17–5:2; 6:10–20; Colossians 3:1–17; 1 Timothy 1:18.

166: Stress

A few years ago an interesting study was conducted in India. They were interested in studying the difference between the high energy and the low energy people. Both kinds of people were doing the same mindless, repetitive task. They were putting fifty matches in a box, sliding the sleeve over the box and placing the finished product on a tray. The situations vacant column described the job as requiring someone to be involved in a two-step pre-ignition phase in a high energy industry.

Themes: Anxiety, Boredom, Work.

Scriptures: Psalms 34:4; 46; 55:22; Luke 12:22–31; Ephesians 6:5–8; Colossians 3:23.

167: Stress

Keith and Colleen are a couple whose family has been under great stress. Shortly after birth, Cynthia, their daughter, developed a serious infection. This led to her becoming profoundly deaf in the first month of her life. At first Keith and his wife responded with the question, 'Why us?' This is the question of any parents who learn that their child is deaf, retarded, blind, disabled, critically ill or injured. Initially Keith and Colleen felt feelings of hopelessness and helplessness. They prayed fervently that baby Cindy would hear and speak. They felt anger and guilt. They wanted prompt, definitive action from God. When what they wanted did not come over the next year or so, they felt disillusionment. Then one night, many months and many prayers later it happened. Keith had been away on a business trip. He was returning on the train in a sleeper car. It was cold and wet. When the train stopped suddenly at a siding Keith woke. He looked out the window to see where he was. He saw a full moon shining behind the cross bars of the railroad crossing. Something forced him to fix his eyes on the sign. Soon the crossing sign became a giant crucifix. He was transfixed by what he saw – and heard. From out of the cross came a brilliant light and a remarkably calm voice that said, 'Don't despair. Out of the misfortune of your daughter will come benefits for many.' Then the voice and the cross disappeared. Keith was left with an experience of God that changed his attitudes and the stress in his family. That happened just over thirty hears ago. Cindy can only hear through lip reading, though she can speak quite well. She became an excellent athlete and has been through tertiary education. Cindy is involved in recreation and health sports for people with disabilities. God turned around a crippling source of stress for Keith and Colleen by giving them peace and a way of carrying the load.

Themes: Anger, Guilt, Illness, Peace, Suffering.

Scriptures: Job; Psalm 23; 2 Corinthians 1:3–7; 4:7–12; 7:6; Colossians 1:24; James 1:2–4.

168: Stress

Phil Edge is the welfare officer for the Victorian Police Association in Australia. Recently he told his story to a conference on stress. He said, 'I don't recall driving home that particular day, but after arriving home and wandering around like a proverbial lost sheep for some time, I decided to sit down and watch a golf tournament on TV.' Then he said, 'It wasn't until I saw something wet on my hand a short time later that I realized I was crying uncontrollably. When I rang the doctor and told him what had happened his response was, "Now do you believe that you are suffering from stress?"

Themes: Anxiety, Illness, Work, Worry.

Scriptures: Psalms 34:4; 46; 55:22; Luke 12:22–31; Ephesians 6:5–8; Colossians 3:23.

169: Substitution

At one stage, in India, the British were fighting a native monarch called Tippo Saib. In one of the battles, several English officers were taken prisoner. Among them was a man named Baird who had been severely wounded. One day, an Indian officer brought in fetters to be put on each of the prisoners. The wounded Baird was not exempt from the ordeal even though he was suffering from pain and weakness. A grey haired officer said to the native official, 'Don't think you're putting chains upon that wounded young man.' But the Indian said, 'There are just as many pairs of fetters as there are prisoners and every pair must be worn.'

'Then,' said the officer, 'put two pairs on me. I'll wear his as well as my own.' Baird lived to regain his freedom, but the generous friend died in prison.

Themes: Courage, Cross, Easter, Encouragement, Jesus – his death, Love, Martyrdom, Persecution, Sacrifice, Suffering.

Scriptures: Psalm 27:14, Isaiah 53; Mark 10:45; Luke 10:27; John 11:50; Romans 3:21–25; 1 Corinthians 13; Galatians 3:13; 1 Timothy 2:6; Hebrews 9:28; 1 Peter 2:24.

170: Substitution

Giuseppe Verdi's opera *Rigoletto* has an interesting ending. Rigoletto, the Duke's jester, has a daughter Gilda who has become the mistress of the Duke. To say the least, the Duke is a ladies' man and is unfaithful to Gilda. She is heartbroken and has lost the will to live, but not her love for the Duke. Rigoletto schemes to get rid of the Duke. Rather than see the Duke killed, Gilda, dressed as a man, is killed in his place.

Rigoletto had arranged to dump the sack with the body in it into the river. When he hears the Duke still singing inside the inn he frantically cuts open the sack to find his dying daughter inside the bag instead of the Duke.

Themes: Atonement, Courage, Cross, Easter, Encouragement, Jesus – his death, Love, Martyrdom, Persecution, Sacrifice, Suffering.

Scriptures: Psalm 27:14; Isaiah 53; Mark 10:45; Luke 10:27; Romans 3:21–25; John 11:50; 1 Corinthians 13; Galatians 3:13; 1 Timothy 2:6; Hebrews 9:28; 1 Peter 2:24.

171: Suffering

In the saga of the Cherokee people's *Trail of Tears*, the Cherokee nation, trying to keep peace and self-pride, reluctantly agreed to move from North Carolina to the Oklahoma Indian Territory. It really was a trail of tears as they marched because, between the sickness and the starvation, half of the Cherokee nation didn't make it alive. Funeral after funeral was held for young and old alike. It is one of the sad and grief-filled stories of the injustices against the Native Americans.

There is an interesting side story to this agonizing tale. Every single one of the soldiers assigned as guards for this forced march were converted along the way. No one could remain unmoved or go untouched by the plight of these people as they resolutely followed and left their home for another. But that was not what brought about the conversion of these guards. The guards were all converted by a song that the Cherokee people sang over and over again in the midst of their personal and national tragedy. The title of that song contains all the words that there are. It is a simple song with a simple message, 'What can we do for you Jesus? What can we do for you?'

Themes: Evangelism, Light, Persecution, Singing, Tragedy, Witness.

Scriptures: Job; Matthew 5:12, 16; 13:43; Acts 5:41; 9:4–5; 14:22; Romans 5:3; 12:12; 2 Corinthians 1:3–7; 11:16–23; Philippians 1:29; 3:10; Colossians 3:24; 1 Thessalonians 1:6; 2 Timothy 3:12; Hebrews 2:18; 4:15; 12:3, 5, 11; 13:13; James 1:2–4; 1 Peter 1:6–7; 2:21; 4:1–2, 12–16; 5:9.

172: Suffering

Somewhere Helen Rosevere writes:

> In 1981 I had breast cancer. I was thirty-six years old. My mother had died thirty-two years earlier at the age of thirty-six with breast cancer. In 1983 I had a second mastectomy and learned that my husband was having a mid-life crisis affair. In 1986, our bright beautiful eighteen-year-old son took his life. No warning. No sign that he'd been unhappy. My husband and I were at home, when he quietly hanged himself in the basement. In 1988, after twenty-one years of what I thought was a good marriage, my husband moved in with his Friday night rendezvous. Because of all the Hell we'd been through I was certain that nothing could break us apart. When he left me the pain was gut-wrenching, but I got through it. How have I overcome all this grief in my life? It was due to the help that I received in the loving support of my church, my family and my friends, but above all it was my belief in the presence of God in my life.

Themes: Cancer, God – his presence, Grief, Marriage, Mid-life crisis, Separation.

Scriptures: Job; Matthew 5:12; Acts 5:41; 9:4–5; 14:22; Romans 5:3; 8:17–18; 12:12; 1 Corinthians 12:26–27; 2 Corinthians 1:3–7; Galatians 6:2; Philippians 1:29; 3:10; 1 Thessalonians 1:6; 2 Timothy 3:12; Hebrews 2:18; 4:15; 12:3, 5, 11; 13:13; James 1:2–4; 1 Peter 1:6–7; 2:21; 4:1–2, 12–16; 5:9.

173: Service

Leonard Bernstein was one of America's greatest composers and conductors, directing and conducting the New York Philharmonic Orchestra from 1958 to 1969. His musical *West Side Story* brought him wide acclaim.

An admirer once asked Bernstein what was the hardest instrument to play. He replied without hesitation: 'Second fiddle. I can always get plenty of first violins, but to find one who plays second fiddle with as much enthusiasm, or second French horn, or second flute, now that's a problem. And yet if no one plays second, we have no harmony.'

Themes: Body of Christ, Ego, Envy, Fruit of the Spirit, Humility, Jealousy, Parable – Pharisee and the Tax Collector, Pride, Spirit – fruit of.

Scriptures: Psalm 5:5; Proverbs 11:2; 15:25; 16:18–19; Mark 7:22; Luke 18:9–14; Romans 1:30; 12:1–8; 1 Corinthians 12:12–31; Galatians 5:16–22; Ephesians 4:4–16; 1 John 2:15–17.

174: Sunday

William Wilberforce was a member of the English Parliament in the early years of last century. He became famous for convincing Parliament to outlaw slavery in the British Empire.

It took Wilberforce twenty years of hard work to

construct the coalition of law-makers that eventually passed the antislavery bills. The spiritual strength and moral courage of Wilberforce had to be – and was – immense.

There was an important ingredient in his life. It is shown in an incident in 1801. In that year it was rumoured that Wilberforce was to be among the candidates for a Cabinet post. He found himself most anxious to gain the appointment. For days it grabbed at his conscious mind, forcing aside everything else. By his own admission, the rising ambition was crippling his life. Sunday brought the cure.

This is what Wilberforce wrote in his journal at the end of that week of furious fantasizing and temptations to politic for position; 'Blessed be to God for the day of rest and religious occupation wherein earthly things assume their true size. Ambition is stunted.' Wilberforce had discovered the importance of Sunday.

Themes: Ambition, Courage, Refreshment, Rest, Sabbath, Slavery.

Scriptures: Exodus 20:8–11; 31:12–17; Leviticus 23:3; Nehemiah 13:15–22; Isaiah 58:13–14; Jeremiah 17:19–23; Mark 2:27; Romans 12:3–8; Revelation 1:10.

175: Surrender

In 1967, Paul Stanley was an infantry company commander in the Vietnam War. He saw Viet Cong soldiers surrender many times.

On one occasion, after the enemy had withdrawn, Paul came across several soldiers surrounding a wounded Viet Cong. He was shot through the leg. He was hostile, yet helpless. He threw mud and kicked with his good leg when anyone went near him. Paul joined the circle and looked down at the soldier who was losing blood fast. He looked into his face and saw a sixteen or seventeen-year-old boy.

Paul unbuckled his pistol and belt and hand grenades so he couldn't grab them. Then speaking gently, he moved toward him. The helpless soldier stared fearfully at Paul as he knelt down. But he allowed Paul to slide his arms under him and pick him up.

As Paul walked along with him towards the helicopter, the young man began to cry and hold him tight. He kept looking at Paul and squeezing him tighter. They climbed into the helicopter and took off. During the ride, the young captive sat on the floor, clinging to Paul's leg. He had never ridden in a helicopter before. He fixed his eyes on Paul who smiled reassuringly and put his hand on the fellow's shoulder.

After landing, Paul picked him up and walked towards the medical tent. As they crossed the field, Paul felt the tenseness leave the boy's body. His tight grasp loosened. His eyes softened and he leant his head against Paul's chest. The fear and resistance were gone. He had finally surrendered.

Themes: Acceptance, Enemies – love for, Jesus – work of, Fear, Parable – Good Samaritan, Parable – Lost Sheep, Reconciliation, Rescue, Salvation.

Scriptures: Isaiah 64:8; Malachi 1:6; 2:10; Luke 10:25–37; 11:1–4; 15:1–7, 8–10, 11–32; 19:10; John 10:1–18; 20:17; Romans 5:10; 8:17; 11:28; Galatians 3:26; Philippians 3:18; Colossians 1:21–22; Hebrews 12:9.

176: Temptation

Handley Paige was a pioneer flyer in the early days of aviation. On one of his long flights in which he was testing an aeroplane, he came down on a field near a city in India; he had to take some rest. When he came back and took off, he had only been flying a short time when he heard a gnawing sound behind him. He knew at once what had happened – a rat had got on board his plane while he was grounded and was gnawing.

Now those were the days when aeroplanes were not what they are now; that rat could easily have chewed through something that could keep Paige from controlling his flight, and could destroy him.

Suddenly a solution occurred to him. He remembered that rats live in low altitudes. So he pointed the nose of the plane upwards and climbed until the air became so thin he could hardly breath. He knew he couldn't go any higher or he would black out, so he levelled off and continued to fly at that altitude.

After a while, he didn't hear the gnawing, but he didn't take any chances. He continued to fly at a high altitude for a long time. When he came down at his next stop, he looked in the back to find a dead rat.

Themes: Character, Enemies, Evil, Life – troubles, Old life, Perseverance, Spiritual battles.

Scriptures: Psalm 1; Romans 6:1–14; 7:14–23; 8:31–39; 1 Corinthians 4:16; 9:24–27; 16:13; 2 Corinthians 10:1–6; Galatians 5:16–26; Ephesians 3:16–17; 4:17–5:2; 6:10–20; Colossians 3:1–17; 1 Timothy 1:18.

177: *Testimony*

One Sunday in a particular church, there was a woman who sang in the choir. She was a former drug addict, who had the HIV virus.

During the service she told the story of how she came to Christ. She described in raw detail the horrors of her former life.

A street person named Roger stood at the back listening closely. After church he approached John, one of the ministry team. John was tired and knew that Roger was going to hit him for money. When Roger got close, the smell took John's breath away: a mixture of urine, sweat, garbage and alcohol.

After a few words, John reached into his pocket and pulled out a couple of dollars for him. John's posture must have communicated the message, 'Here's some money. Now get out of here.' For, Roger looked intently at John, put his finger in his face and said,

'Look, I don't want your money. I'm going to die out there. I want the Jesus this girl talked about.'

Themes: Acceptance, Conversion, Drugs, Money.

Scriptures: John 2:23; 4:1–42, 53; 6:2, 26; 10:42; 11:45; 12:9, 37; Acts 13:4–12; 14:8–18; 16:16–18; 19:20; 20:7–12; 28:7–10; Romans 4:21; 15:19; 1 Corinthians 2:1–5; 2 Corinthians 12:9–10; 1 Thessalonians 1:5, 9.

178: Testimony – David Cornish

David is a Christian and was in midlife when his work was obviously slipping. In a letter to a friend he wrote, '. . . I found myself in a real pit of darkness and despair, being hopelessly depressed and unable to find any solution.' David went away on three months long-service leave. He came back worse than when he left.

The doctor put him on drugs to calm him down and he went away to a rest home for a week. His wife set herself to pray for David in every spare moment she had. When he came back he found his wife really glowing, really radiant. At 4 am on the morning David was to return, she had suddenly awakened to find the Lord at her bedside, invisibly but really there. And the power of God seemed to flow through and through her as she silently worshipped. After two hours she rose, walking on air. That night David heard all this and his wife prayed for him. 'Then,' he said, 'she laid her hand on my head, and prayed . . . it was as though a great wave of . . . liquid love . . . broke over me, and as it did so, it seemed to wash me clean . . . all the depression, guilt, fear, hopelessness . . . and even much of the awful drugged feeling. I felt like a new man. And that night I slept like a baby!'

David concludes: 'We have found the coming of the Holy Spirit . . . does *not* make life easy . . . it makes life fifty times more difficult, but, praise the Lord he gives fifty times more grace.'

Themes: Depression, Despair, Grace, Healing – inner, Holy Spirit – filling, Inner healing, Mid-life, Pentecost, Refreshment, Renewal.

Scriptures: Joel 2:28; Acts 2:1–4; 3:19–20; 4:31; 9:17; 13:52; Ephesians 5:18.

179: Testimony – Ted Dexter

Ted Dexter was the captain of the English cricket team. He would have worked under immense pressure with the eyes and hopes of millions of people on him. He has turned his life over to God. Ted said this: 'In June 1967 some very good news happened to me. Having attempted to fight my own battles for too long with so little success, I have put my trust in Jesus Christ, and am praying that he will give me the strength I otherwise lack. There's a new side to my life now!'

Themes: Conversion, Evangelism, Joy.

Scriptures: Psalm 100; Luke 10:20; John 15:11; Acts 2:1–42; 9:1–19; 10:34–48; 1 Thessalonians 5:16–18.

180: Testimony – Chris Frager

Chris Frager's father left home when she was six. She missed him badly. They'd had some good times together. Her mother was left with her and her three sisters, but couldn't cope, and Chris was sent to a Children's Home until she was twelve. She longed to have a normal home again and especially a dad.

She was excited when she heard that her mother was marrying again as that would mean she could have a stepdad. But things did not work out. She came to hate the man. One day she told him so. He flew into a cold rage and yelled at her, 'Get out!' The next day she was thrown out.

Chris was seventeen and did not know where to go or what to do. It was school holidays so she looked for a job. Chris found a job in a hospital where she could live in. Helping dying people took her mind off her problems, and all that was going on inside her. When school started again she had to find somewhere else to live because she went back to working only weekends. Sometimes she was hungry and had to miss school because she did not have the money for the bus fare.

There were some Christians at her school. They started to make friends with her. Exams were looming and they said they were going to have a prayer meeting and breakfast on the beach one morning, and they asked Chris to go. She thought a bit of heavenly help for exams wouldn't go astray and in any case, a free meal was what appealed most. The event blew Chris's mind. The group cared for her.

The crunch came one Sunday night when she was invited to church. It was a song which broke her up. The song was about God's love and Chris cried and cried. That night when she got home she thought a lot about God. 'What if he is real? What if he really does love me?' she asked herself. It seemed that God was the one solution to the mess she was in and the one who could heal all the hurts from her past. So she said this to God, 'God, if you're real I want to know it when I wake up in the morning. If not, I'm going to forget about you.' When she woke up in the morning, God was just there. She was excited about the reality of God's presence. At school that day she told all her friends that she was a Christian, even though she didn't know what that meant. But, from that time her life was changed as nothing else or no one else could change it.

Chris is now married to Rusty Frager. They write, sing and record songs under the Rhema record label.

Themes: Change, Conversion, Divorce, Family, God – his existence, God – his love, God – his presence, Parenting, Rejection.

Scriptures: Psalm 100; Luke 10:20; John 3:16; 15:11; Acts 2:1–42; 9:1–19; 10:34–48; 2 Corinthians 5:17; Ephesians 5:21–6:3; Colossians 3:18–21; 1 Thessalonians 5:16–18.

181: Testimony – Mitsuo Fuchida

It was 7 December 1941. As Mitsuo Fuchida's plane climbed steeply, he switched the radio frequency to his home aircraft carrier. Jubilantly he cried, 'Tora! Tora! Tora!' ('Tiger! Tiger! Tiger!') which was the code signal for the successful attack he had just lead on Pearl Harbour.

Having ascertained that the main force of the American Pacific Fleet of eight warships was at anchor in Pearl Harbour, Mitsuo had lifted the curtain of warfare by despatching that cursed Order No. 1 'Whole squadron, plunge into attack!'

He described his feeling. 'My heart was ablaze with joy for my success in getting the whole main force of American Pacific Fleet in hand, and I put my whole effort into the war that followed, the result of which was that misery which is clear to everyone today.' He said that in the following four years of war he faced death several times. But he was miraculously saved every time.

After the war, and twenty-five years of Navy service, he retired to farming. As he lived in close relation to the earth he was gradually led to think of the presence of God, the Creator. He also arrived at the conclusion that the only way for the Japanese to survive and prosper would be for the people to become thoroughly peaceful. He began to write a book, *No More Pearl Harbour*.

He said this, 'As my writing progressed, I came to realize that in my appeal for "No More Pearl Harbour" there must be an assurance of the transformation of hatred among mankind to true brotherly love. So long as mankind remained in opposition to one another within the frame of nationality, the only consequence could be the destruction of civilization.' In the midst of these thoughts Mitsuo went to a Pocket Testament League meeting at Shibuya railway station in Tokyo. There he was handed a pamphlet, *I was a War Prisoner of Japan*. Mitsuo was captivated by the story. In it Jacob DeShazer told how one day he came to feel a strong desire to read the Bible. Jacob recalled he had heard about Christianity which could transform human hatred to true brotherly love. In turn, Mitsuo decided to buy and read a Bible.

Here is what he later said:

> Before covering the first thirty pages my mind was strongly impressed and captivated.
> This is it! I was strongly convinced. I concluded that the true realization of *No More Pearl Harbour* was no other than to expect Christ's Second Coming and to endeavour to prepare men from all over the world worthy of welcoming Christ's return.
>
> As a first approach towards this, I was convinced that I should first of all become a good Christian . . . I then opened my heart and accepted Jesus Christ as my personal Saviour on 14 April 1950.

Later Mitsuo said, 'I am still in the early stage of Christian growth, but I feel great joy in my daily Bible reading, and my heart is filled with peace as I kneel down to pray.'

Themes: Conversion, God – creator, Joy, Love one another.

Scriptures: Psalms 32; 34; 100; 121; Matthew 10:16–20; Mark 11:25; Luke 10:20; 18:9–14; John 14:6; 15:11; Acts 2:1–42; 9:1–19; 10:34–48; Philippians 2:3–11; 1 Thessalonians 5:16–18; 2 Timothy 3:16; Hebrews 13:5–6; James 1:5.

182: Testimony – Ignatius

The great Christian Bishop of Antioch, Ignatius, was born about the time Jesus rose from the dead. We know little about his life except that in the year 107 AD ten armed soldiers escorted him from Antioch to Rome. This was no holiday trip. He was on the way to be thrown to the lions. Here is what he wrote to some friends.

> From Syria to Rome I am fighting with wild beasts by land and sea, by night and day, bound to ten leopards, that is, a bunch of soldiers, whose usage grows still harsher when they are treated well. Yet through their unjust activities I am more truly learning discipleship. 'Yet I am not justified by this' [1 Corinthians 4:4]. May I have joy of the beasts that are prepared for me . . .

Then he says that if the lions are a bit slow he will entice them to hurry up and start eating him. He goes on.

> Excuse me. I know what is best for me. Now I am beginning to be a disciple. May nothing seen or unseen distract me, so I may reach to Jesus Christ. Let there come on me fire and cross and conflicts with wild beasts, wrenching of bones, mangling of limbs, crushing of the whole body . . .

Themes: Martyrdom, Persecution, Suffering.

Scriptures: Psalms 34:1; 71:6; Hosea 14:2; Matthew 5:12; Romans 5:3–5; 14:7–8; 2 Corinthians 5:15; Galatians 2:20; 6:9; Ephesians 5:20; Philippians 1:21; 4:12; Hebrews 10:34; 13:15; James 1:2–4; 1 Peter 1:7; 2:5.

183: Testimony – Sakae Kobayashi

Sakae Kobayashi was selected to be a Japanese suicide or kamikaze pilot. Like all kamikaze pilots his task was to fly a plane filled with explosives and make a suicidal dive on a target: usually a ship. The day came for his flight, 14 August, 1945. He sat in the plane waiting for orders to take off. While the engine was warming a ground crew man ran to tell him that Japan had just surrendered.

This is what Sakae said, 'I went home despondent and bitter. My home had been burned, and my mother and grandmother killed. There was no food and no work.'

Later Sakae found work in an oil refinery. There he met a Christian girl who led him to Christ. Then Sakae had this to say, 'I discovered newness of life which only Christ can bring.'

Themes: Conversion, Evangelism, Life – purpose, Renewal, Witness.

Scriptures: Luke 10:20; John 8:31–36; 15:11; Acts 2:1–42; 9:1–19; 10:34–48; Romans 14:7–8; Galatians 2:20.

184: Testimony – Rosario

Rosario is a woman from Peru. She was a terrorist, a brute of a woman who was an expert in several martial arts. In her terrorist activities she had killed twelve policemen.

She had heard a little of the story of Jesus and was incensed at the Christian message. When she heard that Luis Palau was conducting a Christian meeting in Lima she set out to kill Palau.

She made her way into the stadium where Palau was speaking. As she sat there trying to work out how she was going to get close to the speaker she began to listen to the message. Instead of shooting Palau she met Jesus.

Ten years later Luis Palau met Rosario for the first time. In those years she had assisted in planting five churches and had founded an orphanage that houses over 1,000 children.

Themes: Church planting, Conversion, Crusades, Evangelism.

Scriptures: Mark 1:14–15; Luke 4:18–19; Acts 2:1–42; 3:12–26; 4:8–12; 5:29–32; 10:34–48; 13:1–3, 16–41; 14:15–17; 17:22–31.

185: Testimony – Bilquis Sheik

Bilquis Sheik was a high-born Muslim. Her life collapsed when her husband, a high-ranking official in Pakistan, left her. She retreated to the countryside looking for peace. But she did not find it. As she read the Koran she found many references to the prophet Jesus. Out of curiosity she obtained a Bible and began to read it. She found some parts quite compatible with the Koran but in other places there was a clash.

Then Bilquis started to dream. One of the dreams was

about a perfume salesman bringing her a golden jar. His perfume glimmered like liquid crystal. He placed the jar by her bed. 'This will spread throughout the world,' he said. She woke up to find her Bible in the place where the jar had been in the dream. She found some missionaries who interpreted the dream for her. She became a Christian and is living in the USA.

Themes: Bible, Dreams, Marriage, Peace, Separation.

Scriptures: Daniel 2:1–49; Matthew 8:5–13; 9:27–31; Mark 1:29–31, 40–44; 2:1–12; 3:1–6; 5:24–34; 7:31–37; 8:22–26; 10:46–52; Luke 13:1–17; John 4:46–54; 9:1–34; 14:1–6; James 5:14–15.

186: Testimony – Ying Gao

Ying Gao was an eleven-year-old child when the Cultural Revolution began. Her parents held high positions in the communist party, but were soon accused by the Red Guards of being 'capitalist'. They were forced out of their home to perform manual labour.

For Ying Gao, who had become an enthusiastic member of the Red Guards, this was the ultimate disgrace, and she denounced her parents both at home and in public. Less than a year later she herself was expelled from the Red Guards because of her 'bad family'. The family was reunited when she was fifteen, but the hurts were too deep to be reconciled and in any case they were again separated.

Ying Gao was just one of 15 million young people sent to perform manual labour at that time.

By 1976, the Revolution's tenth year, Ying Gao and millions of others had begun to question the truth of the Revolution. She said, 'After the fall of Mao and the "Gang of Four" everything was plain to me and I felt guilty because I had done many wrong things. I became very depressed. I began to look for something to believe in. I had heard about Christianity from western novelists, such as Victor Hugo, and I had the impression that Christianity told people to do good – otherwise I knew nothing.'

In 1980 Ying Gao attended a re-opened Beijing church where a friend's father was a pastor. The first sermon she heard was on reconciliation and being born again. She said, 'These words touched a central part of my heart.'

On her second visit Ying Gao obtained a Bible and began to study it. 'Finally I realized this was exactly what I had been searching for all my life.' Ying Gao's father had died and attempts to be reconciled to her mother failed. 'She decided to stop being my mother when I became a Christian,' said Ying Gao. However, at the time of the Tiananmen Square massacre and just a year before her mother died of cancer, the two were tearfully reconciled.

Today the Rev Ying Gao serves the largest church in Beijing. She said, 'Our needs are for prayer for our pastors – that they will be able to provide nourishment for Christians and not disappoint those who come to the church seeking truth.'

Themes: Bible, Born again, Communication, Reconciliation.

Scriptures: Psalms 32; 34; 100; 121; Matthew 10:16–20; Mark 11:25; Luke 10:20; 18:9–14; John 3:10; 14:6; 15:11; Acts 2:1–42; 9:1–19; 10:34–48; Philippians 2:3–11; 1 Thessalonians 5:16–18; 2 Timothy 3:16; Hebrews 13:5–6; James 1:5.

187: Tithing

Brian and Kayann were thinking about becoming Christians. One day Kayann said to a friend, 'We can't become Christians because I've heard Christians have to give a tenth of their money to the Church. We can't do that because the bathroom needs tiling.'

The friend put it to Kayann that she would discover that if they became Christians and found that God was asking them to give a tenth of their money to him, they would still have money left over for the tiles.

It may have been a year later, after they had become Christians and were giving a tenth of their money to the Lord, Kayann and the friend were talking about this conversation and Kayann asked the friend to go and have a look at the bathroom. It was beautifully tiled. That family praised – and indeed still are praising God for his goodness.

Themes: Giving, God – his care, God – his provision, Materialism, Money, Offerings, Sacrificial giving, Wealth.

Scriptures: Psalm 112:9; Isaiah 55:10–11; Malachi 3:8–10; Mark 10:17–31; 12:41–44; Luke 19:1–10; Acts 4:32–37; 2 Corinthians 8; 9; 1 Timothy 6:17–19; Hebrews 13:5.

188: Tradition

Years ago in Russia, a Tsar came upon a lonely sentry standing at attention in a secluded corner of the palace garden. 'What are you guarding?' asked the Tsar. 'I don't know. The captain ordered me to this post,' the sentry replied.

The Tsar called the captain. His answer: 'Written regulations specify a guard was to be assigned to that area.' The Tsar ordered a search to find out why. The archives finally yielded the reason. Years before, Catherine the Great had planted a rose bush in that corner. She ordered a sentry to protect it for that evening.

One hundred years later, sentries were still guarding the now barren spot.

Themes: Change, Humour, Law, Regulations.

Scriptures: Matthew 5:21–48; Mark 7:1–23; Romans 3:20; 4:14; 6:14–15; 2 Corinthians 5:17; Galatians 2:16; 3:1–14, 18; 5:18; Philippians 3:9.

189: Treasure Found

Somewhere in New England or Upstate New York, late in 1988, there was a clearance sale of unclaimed property. A man bought a painting for $1,000. The painting was in sorry condition, but he thought it might be worth something, perhaps $1,500. So he took the painting to New York.

The painting measured about two metres by just over two metres. It would not fit in his van. So, with some rope, he tied it on the roof of the van. It was not the kind of painting one would take to the luxurious auction houses in Park Avenue so he dropped it off at Christie's East on 67th Street where collectibles were sold. He told an attendant that he would accept as little as $1,500 for his find.

Ian Kennedy was Christie's Old Masters' expert. When he saw the picture he knew they had a fabulous picture by Dosso Dossi, one of the better Italian Renaissance painters. It was called *An Allegory of Fortune*, commissioned by Isabella d'Este in the Court of Mantua and painted somewhere between 1530 and 1545, but it had disappeared during the last century.

The painting went on sale in Christie's Old Masters auction on 11 January, 1989. It was expected to sell for $600,000 to $800,000.

However, London dealers Hazlitt, Gooden & Fox bought it – dirt, damage and all – for $4 million. It was a record for the artist. Most of the $4 million went to the unidentified man who found it.

Then, two months later, the picture was sold again. This time the Paul Getty Museum purchased the Dosso from the dealers at an undisclosed price.

But the picture was still in a distressing state of repair. Andrea Rothe, Getty's conservator of paintings, thought at first it was hopeless to try to restore the picture. One leg of the male figure had been punctured in several places, either during the trip to New York or the warehouse sales. A horizontal row of chips across the centre of the canvas indicated that, at some point many years ago, the canvas had probably been attached by loops to a horizontal crossbar to prevent sagging when it was hung at an angle. Glue used in this process eventually had contracted and caused small bits of pigment to fall off. In addition, the painting was so dirty and the background so dark that many of its subtleties were lost.

The restoration turned out to be a three-year project including extensive study, and Andrea Rothe finished cleaning the painting only to make a time-consuming discovery. The dark brown background had been sloppily applied, and appeared to be a flat coat of paint added later to cover cracks. This addition had to go – microscopic bit by microscopic bit. Andrea said, 'It was a slow, tedious process – really mind-boggling.' But her work paid off. The original, warm grey background that emerged lends the picture a haunting, atmospheric tone.

She repaired holes, filled cracks, restored losses of paint and gave the painting a coat of varnish. The result is dramatic, but visitors at the Museum in Malibu will only see the impact of the finished work: a massive pair of luminous pink-skinned figures who are bathed in eerie moonlight.

Themes: Gospel – its value, Kingdom of God, Parable – Pearl of Great Price, Parable – Treasure.

Scriptures: Matthew 13:44–46; Mark 6:1–6; Luke 4:22–30; John 1:11–12; 2 Corinthians 4:7.

190: Trinity

Ali Sougou was a Muslim in a Muslim country. After he was converted to Christianity he was arrested and sent directly to prison. He was put in a cell which was so small he could not even kneel down; he had to lean on the wall to sleep. He was fed nothing but rice full of salt and just once a day.

After three months he was taken to a special court arranged by Muslim leaders. They said they did not want him to explain himself or to ask him questions. He was told that he had a choice of three punishments. Ali started to tremble a bit. One choice was to be imprisoned for ever. The second was to be shot. The third was to be deported from the country. As Ali was a family man with eight children and two grandchildren it was a very difficult decision. He had nothing to say. But he felt somebody come from behind, put hands on his shoulders and pull him down. He went down, closed his eyes and prayed loudly. He said, 'Lord Jesus, here I am. I need your answer for these people, and I ask this in your precious name. Amen.'

The whole gathering stood up. They started shouting, 'You people, this man is foolish; let him go away.' So they released him.

The first person Ali led to Christ was a police inspector. He was the one who was sent to watch him. This man came to know the Lord after Ali gave him a New Testament to read. One Sunday the policeman came to Ali and asked him a question. 'Brother I want to ask you a very, very important question. I want to know God the Father, God the Son, and God the Holy Spirit. Do you believe in three gods?'

'No, just one God,' Ali said. Then Ali asked him a question. 'Brother, tell me, what is your work?

He said, 'I am a police officer.'

'Are you married?' continued Ali.

'Oh, yes, I'm married.'

'Have you got children?' Ali went on.

'Oh, yes, I have two children,' he replied.

Then Ali said, 'In the morning when you are in your office, do they call you inspector? Does your wife call you husband? And do your children call you Daddy? But, you are only one person. You are a police officer, a husband, and a father.'

The police officer then asked Ali if he could become a Christian.

Themes: Conversion, Evangelism, Stephen, Testimony, Witness.

Scriptures: Matthew 28:19; Luke 10:20; John 8:31–36; 14:16; 15:11; Acts 2:1–42; 6:8–8:3; 9:1–19; 10:34–48; Romans 14:7–8; 2 Corinthians 13:14; Galatians 2:20; 4:6; 1 John 5:7.

191: Urgency

Ebenezer Wooton was an earnest but eccentric evangelist. Many years ago he was conducting a series of summer evening services on the village green at Lidford Brook. The last meeting had been held; the crowd was melting away; and the evangelist was engaged in taking down the marquee. All at once a young fellow approached him and asked, casually rather than earnestly,

'Mr. Wooton, what must I do to be saved?' The preacher took the measure of the man.

'Too late!' he said, in a matter-of-fact kind of way, glancing up from a somewhat obstinate tent peg with which he was struggling. 'Too late, my friend, too late!'

The young man was startled.

'Oh, don't say that, Mr. Wooton!' he pleaded, a new note coming into his voice.

'Surely it isn't too late just because the meetings are over?'

'Yes, my friend,' exclaimed the evangelist, dropping the cord in his hand, straightening himself up, and looking right into the face of his questioner, 'It's too late! You want to know what you must *do* to be saved, and I tell you that you're hundreds of years too late! The work of salvation is done, completed, *finished*! It was finished on the Cross; Jesus said so the last breath that he drew! What more do you want?'

Themes: Evangelism, Grace alone, Salvation, Works.

Scripture: Romans 1:16–3:20; 5:2; 10:9; 2 Corinthians 4:13; Galatians 5:6; Ephesians 2:1–10; Phlippians 1:29.

192: Value – of people

The story is told of Muretus, a wandering scholar, very learned and very poor. During his wanderings around ancient Rome, Muretus fell ill and was taken to the place where the destitute were kept. The doctors were discussing his case in Latin, but they did not know that he was a scholar and that he understood the doctors' Latin. They were saying that he was a poor creature of value to no one, and that it was hopeless and unnecessary to expend care and money or attention to such a worthless one. Muretus looked up and answered in their own Latin: 'Call no man worthless for whom Christ died.'

Themes: Care – for others, God – his love, Materialism, Parable – Lost Coin, Parable – Lost Sheep, Parable – Prodigal Son, Poverty, Wealth.

Scriptures: Psalms 34; 91; 118; Matthew 6:19–21, 24–34; 10:28; Mark 10:17–31; Luke 8:22–25; 12:1–12; 15:1–7, 8–10, 11–32; 19:1–10; John 11:25–26; 1 Timothy 6:10; 2 Timothy 1:7; Hebrews 13:5–6.

193: Victory

On Sunday evening 18 June 1915, a few kilometres south of Brussels in Belgium, the battle of Waterloo was over. The British had won. Wellington needed to send news of his victory to London. His men set up a series of line-of-sight communication stations and a coded message was sent. But, only the first part of the message got through. Half way through sending the message the fog set in and the signallers could not see each other. All the English received was the terrible news, 'Wellington defeated . . . ' However, later the fog lifted and the whole message could get through, 'Wellington defeated Napoleon at Waterloo.'

Themes: Death, Defeat, Easter, Good news, Resurrection.

Scriptures: Mark 1:1; 16:1–8; Luke 24:1–12; John 20:1–31 Romans 1:3–4; 1 Corinthians 15; 2 Corinthians 13:4; Ephesians 1:19–20.

194: Vision

According to a Native American legend, the chief of a tribe encamped at the base of the mountain was dying. He summoned his three sons and said, 'I am about to die, and one of you will succeed me as chief. I want you to climb our holy mountain and bring back something beautiful. The one whose gift is most outstanding will become the new chief.'

After several days the sons returned. The first brought a flower which was extremely rare and beautiful. The second brought a stone which was colourful, smooth and round, having been polished by rain and wind. The third son said, 'Father, I have brought nothing back. As I stood on top of our holy mountain, I saw that the other side was a beautiful land filled with green pastures and a crystal lake and I had a vision of where our tribe could go for a better life. I was so overwhelmed by what I saw and what I was thinking that I could not bring anything back.'

And the old chief replied, 'You shall be our chief, for you have brought us a gift of vision for a better future.'

Themes: Future, Leadership, Parable – Talents.

Scriptures: Proverbs 29:18; Luke 19:11–27.

195: Waiting

In 1870 a young lieutenant in Prussia went off to war. As he left, he told his girlfriend that he would return and they could get married. The next year, the war with France was over. The victorious Prussian troops returned triumphantly through the streets of Berlin. And Julie stood by the gate waiting for her lover to return. 'He must come, he said he would!' she kept saying. In fact, for forty years, day after day, in all weathers she waited for him to return. One day she became ill at the spot where she waited each day. She had to be taken to hospital where she died. Her soldier never did return.

Themes: Hope, Love, Parable – Prodigal Son, Second Coming, Trust.

Scriptures: Luke 15:11–32; 1 Corinthians 5:5; 15:12–34; 2 Corinthians 1:14; 1 Thessalonians 4:13–5:11; 2 Thessalonians 2:2; Hebrews 9:28; 2 Peter 3:10, 12; Revelation 16:14.

196: Weakness

Alexander Solzhenitsyn, the Russian dissident, was working twelve hours a day at hard labour. He had lost his family and had been told by the doctors in the Gulag that he had terminal cancer. One day he thought, 'There is no use going on. I'm soon going to die anyway.' Ignoring the guards, he dropped his shovel, sat down, and rested his head in his hands.

He felt a presence next to him and looked up and saw an old man he had never seen before, and would never see again. The man took a stick and drew a cross in the sand in front of Solzhenitsyn. It reminded him that there is a Power in the world that is greater than any empire or government, a Power that could bring new life to his situation. He picked up his shovel and went back to work. A year later Solzhenitsyn was unexpectedly released from prison.

Themes: Cancer, Cross, Encouragement, Persecution, Power – in weakness, Suffering.

Scriptures: Psalms 34:1; 71:6; Hosea 14:2; Matthew 5:12; Acts 11:22–26; 15:41; Romans 5:3–5; 14:7–8, 19; 1 Corinthians 10:23; 2 Corinthians 5:15; 12:1–13; Galatians 2:20; 6:9;

Ephesians 4:29; 5:20; Philippians 1:21; 4:12; 1 Thessalonians 5:11; Hebrews 10:34; 13:15; James 1:2–4; 1 Peter 1:7; 2:5.

197: Wealth

The richest man in the world is the Sultan of Brunei, a small state in north west Borneo. He knows that nothing is beyond his wildest dreams. He took a fancy to playing polo and bought himself 200 of the best ponies in the world. He wanted an Olympic-sized pool, so he built one. He took up golf and had an international standard 18-hole golf course built outside one of his palaces. His fleet of planes is constantly changing. The latest acquisition is a luxury airbus and a Boeing 757. The British Queen has assets of only $11.6 billion. The Sultan of Brunei's assets are estimated to be $37 billion. His annual income alone is greater than the total assets of all but the very richest people on earth. Put simply, his income is equivalent to $7.3 million a day, or $300,000 an hour. Even while he is asleep he is earning $5,000 a minute, or $84 a second.

Themes: Achievement, Generosity, Greed, Life style, Materialism, Money, Parable – Rich Man and Lazarus, Prosperity, Tithing.

Scriptures: Psalm 37:29; Proverbs 1:19; 15:27; 21:26; 29:25; Matthew 5:22; 6:24; Mark 4:18–19; 8:36; 10:17–31; Luke 6:24; 12:16–21; 16:13, 19–31; Ephesians 4:28; 1 Timothy 3:3, 8; 6:10, 17–19.

198: Work

Richard Wurmbrand spent many, many years in communist prisons. He says that those in solitary confinement communicated with each other by tapping Morse code on the walls. He would preach the Gospel in that way. For some light relief they would tell each other jokes. Here is one he heard tapped out on his wall.

Three men sat in a prison and asked each other why they had been arrested. The first said that he was arrested for sabotage because he had come to work five minutes late. The second said that he had been arrested for spying on the company as he had gone to work five minutes early. The third said that he had been arrested because he arrived at work on time, which meant that he must have had connections with the West from where he had got himself a good watch.

Themes: Honesty, Humour, Materialism, Parable – Talents, Prison, Suffering.

Scriptures: Genesis 37:22–24; 39:19–23; 40:1–8; 42:16–19; Judges 16:21–25; 1 Kings 22:27; 2 Chronicles 16:10; 18:26; Nehemiah 3:25; 12:39; Isaiah 42:7; Jeremiah 32:2, 8, 12; 33:1; 37:16, 20, 21; 38:6, 13, 28; Matthew 25:14–30; Acts 16:23–40; 21:27–22:29; 28:30; Romans 12:11; 13:13; 1 Corinthians 4:2; 14:12; 2 Corinthians 6:5; 11:23; Galatians 4:18; 6:9; Ephesians 4:28; 6:5–9, 20; Philippians 1:7, 13, 14, 16, 17; Colossians 1:10; 3:23–24; 4:3, 18; 1 Thessalonians 4:11; 2 Thessalonians 3:10; 1 Timothy 4:12; 2 Timothy 1:16; 2:9, 21; Titus 2:14; Philemon 10, 13; 1 Peter 4:10.

199: Works

The television programme, *The Marathon Monks of Mount Hiei*, was a fascinating account of Tanno-Ajari's successful attempt to complete 1,000 marathons in seven years. This thirty-six-year-old monk made the commitment to walk 27,000 miles under penalty of suicide in order to become a living Buddha.

Behind this astonishing physical exertion lies the theory that, in undergoing such austerity, enlightenment can be obtained without subsequent reincarnation.

As if this gruelling pilgrimage was not enough, a nine-day total fast was imposed after the first 700 trips up and down the mountain. Sleep was denied by the constant repetition of 100,000 mantras during this period, which takes the postulant deity two days beyond medical life expectancy.

The programme traced Tanno's journeyings and mortifications over two years until their completion and his proclamation as a god. As only the seventh man to undergo this experience since 1945, he captivated the public imagination.

Themes: Fasting, Grace, Law, Love, Monks, Reincarnation.

Scripture: Exodus 34:27–28; 2 Samuel 12:16–24; Ezra 8:21; Psalm 69:10; Isaiah 58:5–12; Jeremiah 14:11–12; Zechariah 7:1–14; 8:19; Mark 2:18–22; Romans 1:16–3:20; 5:2, 10:9; 2 Corinthians 4:13; Galatians 5:6; Ephesians 2:1–10; Philippians 1:29.

200: X-rated

Someone had stolen the vicar's bike. He felt sure that one of his parishioners was the thief. So he decided to preach a sermon on the Ten Commandments. When he came to 'Thou shalt not steal,' he made a great deal of the commandment, preaching eloquently about the scourge of theft and the collapse of standards in society. However, when he came to the commandment, 'Thou shalt not commit adultery,' he suddenly remembered where he had left his bike.

Themes: Adultery, Ethics, Humour, Sexuality, Stealing, Ten Commandments, Theft.

Scriptures: Exodus 20:14; Leviticus 20:10; Deuteronomy 5:18; Proverbs 6:32; Jermiah 3:8; 5:7; 13:27; Hosea 2:1–5; Matthew 5:7–8; 19:9; Mark 7:21; 10:11; 19; John 8:1–11; 2 Peter 2:14.

ACKNOWLEDGEMENTS

1. John White, *Eros Defiled: Christian and Sexual Guilt* (Leicester: Inter-Varsity, 1978), p 108.
4. Adapted from 'Safe not Sorry,' The Advertiser (Adelaide, 6 June 1992), 'Magazine', p 5.
5. Adapted from Ed Silvoso, *That None Should Perish* (Ventura: Regal, 1994), p 82.
6. Tony Campolo, *20 Hot Potatoes Christians are Afraid to Touch* (Milton Keynes: Word, 1988), p 107.
7. Adapted from 'To Illustrate . . . ' *Leadership* 15 (#3, 1994), p 48.
9. Tony Campolo, *It's Friday But Sunday's Coming* (Milton Keynes: Word, 1989), p 50.
11. Adapted from 'This is Australia', *The Sower*, the magazine of the Bible Society in Australia, Canberra, No 149 Special Edition 1994, p 5.
13. Elizabeth Berg, 'I Can't Believe You're Here!: A New Mother's Diary,' *Parents* (April 1992), p 98, 102, 104.
14. Adapted from *Parables, Etc.* 14 (#2, April 1994), p 2. (Saratoga Press).
15. Adapted from *Pulpit Resource* 4(#1, 1987), p 9 (Media Corn Associates Inc).
16. Adapted from James Dobson, 'When God Doesn't Make Sense,' *Profamily* 2 (1993–4), pp 6–7 (Focus on the Family Australia).
17. L Griffith, *Barriers to Christian Belief* (London: Hodder and Stoughton, 1967), p 183.
18. John Stott, *Romans: God's Good News for the World* (Downers Grove: IVP, 1994), pp 187–8.
21. From Gordon MacDonald, *Ordering Your Private World* (Crowborough: Highland Books, 1987), pp 103–4.
25. Adapted from David Grayson, *Terror in the Skies: The Inside Story of the World's Worst Air Crashes* (New York: Carol, 1988), Chapter 6.

26. J C Beaglehole (ed.), *The Voyage of the Endeavour 1768–1771: The Journals of Captain James Cook on is Voyages of Discovery* Volume 1 (Cambridge: Cambridge University Press, 1968), pp 167, 173.
29. Adapted from John Wimber, *Power Evangelism* (London: Hodder and Stoughton, 1985), pp 44–6.
30. Adapted from Michael Green, *Evangelism Through the Local Church* (London: Hodder and Stoughton, 1990), p 318.
31. In Kenneth Suirin, *Theology and the Problem of Evil* (Oxford: Blackwell, 1986), p 147.
32. Adapted from John White, *Parents in Pain* (Leicester: Inter-Varsity, 1980), p 162.
33. Adapted from 'To Illustrate . . . ,' *Leadership* 15 (#4, 1994), p 43.
34. Adapted from Peter Wagner, *How to Have a Healing Ministry Without Making Your Church Sick* (Eastbourne: Monarch, 1988), p 151.
35. Adapted from John Wimber, *Power Healing* (London: Hodder and Stoughton, 1986), pp 111–2.
36. Adapted from Guy Chevreau, *Catch the Fire: The Toronto Blessing* (London: Marshall Pickering, 1994), pp 146–9.
38. Adapted from *Encounter* (January, 1993), p 11.
39. William P Wilson 'Hysteria and Demons, Depression and Oppression, Good and Evil,' in John Warwick Montgomery (ed.), *Demon Possession* (Minneapolis: Bethany House, 1976), p 227.
40. Adapted from Ivor Bailey, *Prate, Prattle or Preach* (Melbourne: JBCE, 1987), p 118.
44. Adapted from Stephen M Hooks, 'Our Debt is Paid,' *Decision* (May 1992), pp 31–32.
45. Adapted from Ed and Ruth Silvoso, *Prayer Letter*, (10 April 1994), p 3. (Harvest Evangelism).
47. Adapted from *Pulpit Resource* 4 (#2, 1987), p 10.
49. Adapted from George Carey, *Church in the Market Place* (Eastbourne: Kingsway, 1984), p 132.
50. Adapted from Hudson Taylor, *Retrospect* (London: Overseas Missionary Fellowship, 1974), p 102.
53. Adapted from Michael P Green (ed.), *Illustrations for Biblical Preaching* (Grand Rapids: Baker, 1989), #891.
54. From *Good News Letter* 28 (January 1995), p 10.
56. Used with permission.
57. David Hanes (ed.), *My Path of Prayer* (Worthing: Walter, 1981), p 32 as cited in John Woolmer, *Growing up to Salvation* (London: Triangle/SPCK, 1983), p 132
58. Walter B Knight, *Knight's Treasury of Illustrations* (Grand Rapids: Eerdmans, 1963), p 153.
60. Adapted from Peter Wagner, *Spiritual Power and Church Growth* (London: Hodder and Stoughton, 1986), pp 17–18.

61. Gordon MacDonald, *Rebuilding Your Broken World* (Crowborough: Highland, 1988), p 92.
62. Nick Cavanar, 'When Your Prayers Aren't Answered,' *On Being* (July 1987), p 34.
63. Peter Wagner, *How to Have a Healing Church Without Making Your Church Sick* (Eastbourne: Monarch, 1988), p 213.
64. John White, *When the Spirit Comes With Power* (London: Hodder and Stoughton, 1989), p 122.
65. Adapted from Colin Urquhart, *Anything You Ask* (London: Hodder and Stoughton, 1978), p 1.
66. Eleanor Doan, *Speakers Sourcebook* (Grand Rapids: Zondervan, 1960), p 123.
73. David Lodge, *The British Museum is Falling Down*, (New York: Penguin, 1989), p XVII.
74. Adapted from Raymond Brown, *Be My Disciple* (Basingstoke: Marshall–Pickering, 1992), pp 142–143.
75. Annetta Miller (et al.), 'Stress on the Job,' in *The Bulletin, Newsweek* (26 April 1988), p 86.
76. Herb Miller, *How to Build a Magnetic Church* (Nashville: Abingdon, 1987), p 112.
77. Paul Lee Tan, *Encyclopedia of 7,700 Illustrations: Signs of the Times* (Garland, TX: Bible Communications, 1979), #3489.
78. Adapted from Ian Barclay, 'Hind Sight,' *Church of England Newspaper*, 19 December 1986, p 9.
79. Adapted from Anthony de Mello, *The Prayer of the Frog*, volume 1 (Anand, India: Gujarat Sahitya Prakash, 1992) pp 4–5.
80. Adapted from *Parables, Etc.* 14 (#4, June 1994), p 5.
81. Donald L Deffner, *Seasonal Illustrations for Preaching and Teaching* (San Jose: Resource, 1992), p 150.
82. Adapted from 'To Illustrate . . . ' *Leadership* 15 (#3, 1994), p 49.
83. Adapted from Grayson, *Terror in the Skies*, chapter 8.
84. Robert Fulgham, *It Was On Fire When I Lay Down On It* (London: Grafton/Collins, 1990), p 176.
85. Gordon MacDonald, *Rebuilding Your Broken World* p 27.
87. Adapted from Paul E Holdcroft, *Cyclopedia of Bible Illustrations* (Nashville: Abingdon, 1947), #242.
92. Lorraine Hansberry, *a raisin in the sun*, (London: Methuen, 1960), p 102.
93. Steve Sjogren, 'Loving Your Community to Christ', audio cassette, *Pastor's Update* 51 (1994).
97. 'A Clergyman Set Free from Adultery', *Church of England Newspaper* (17 May, 1985), p 8.
98. A letter to the Editor, *The Australian* (26 February, 1987), p 10.
99. John Stott, *Issues Facing Christians Today* (Basingstoke: Marshall Morgan & Scott, 1984), p 226.

100. Adapted from Silvoso *That None Should Perish*, p 85.
103. *The Independent* 'Magazine' (1 January 1994), p 38.
104. Adapted from *Parables, Etc.* 15 (#1, March 1995), p 1.
105. Adapted from Leighton Ford, *The Christian Persuader* (London: Hodder and Stoughton, 1967), p 37.
106. Adapted from David Watson, *I Believe in the Church* (London: Hodder and Stoughton, 1978), p 103.
107. Adapted from Holdcraft, *Cyclopedia of Bible Illustrations*, #962
108. Adapted from Russ Parker, *The Occult: Deliverance from Evil* (Leicester: Inter-Varsity, 1989), p 31.
110. Adapted from David A Seamands, *Healing for Damaged Emotions* (Amersham: Scripture, 1986), p 16.
113. Adapted from James Dobson, *Dare to Discipline* (Wheaton: Tyndale, 1970), pp 18–19.
114. Adapted from Jim Cymbala, 'Keeping Connected to Spiritual Power', *Leadership* 14 (#4, 1993), pp 70–71.
115. Adapted from Lorna and Michael Bourdeaux *Ten Growing Soviet Churches* (Marc Europe, 1997), pp 142 and 164.
116. Adapted from William Barclay, *The Gospel of Matthew* (Philadelphia: Westminster, 1975), p 280.
119. Adapted from Herb Miller, *How to Build a Magnetic Church* (Nashville: Abingdon, 1987), p 14.
120. Adapted from David Watson, *Discipleship* (London: Hodder and Stoughton, 1981), p 137.
123. Adapted from Hanes (ed.), *My Path of Prayer*, pp 15–16.
124. Adapted from Stuart Robinson, 'The Spiritual Power of Fasting,' in *Renewal* (January 1995), p 34.
125. Adapted from Robinson, 'The Spiritual Power of Fasting,' in *Renewal* (January 1995), p 34–5.
126. Adapted from Knight, *Treasury*, p 275.
127. Adapted from John Wimber, *Power Healing* (London: Hodder and Stoughton, 1986), p 169.
128. Adapted from Richard Foster, *Prayer* (London: Hodder and Stoughton, 1992), p 83.
130. Adapted from Louis Templeman, 'When They Want You to Perform', *Leadership* 12 (#3, 1991), p 32.
134. Adapted from Johnny Dodd, 'A Survivors Guide to Getting Dumped', *The Advertiser* (12 February 1994), 'Weekend' pp 6–7.
136. Adapted from *Encounter* (April, 1993), p 5.
138. Sources: AP, Reuters, AFP, 'Marines rescue downed pilot from Serbs,' *The Australian* (9 June 1995), p 10; Michael Adler (AFP, AP), 'I'm No Hero . . . ,' *The Australian* (12 June 1995), p 9; Gregory Vistica (et al.), 'A Daring Rescue,' *The Bulletin, Newsweek* (20 June 1995), pp 62–73; Francis X Clines, 'Downed US Pilot Rescued in Bosnia in Daring Raid,'

New York Times (9 June 1995), pp A1, A8, A9; Celestine Bohlen, 'Pilot, Back at Base, Thanks God and His Rescue Crews,' *New York Times* (10 June 1995), pp A1, A6; Celestine Bohlen, 'No "Rambo," And 6 Days On the Run,' *New York Times* (11 June 1995), pp A1, A14; Michael Evans, 'Layers of air power . . . ,' *The Times* (London: 9 June 1995), pp 1, 11; Helen Trinca and agencies, 'US hails its all-American hero,' *The Weekend Australian* (10–11 June 1995), pp 1, 13.

142. René Vallery-Rodot, *The Life of Pasteur* (London: Constable & Company, 1920), pp 192–3 and Nesta Pain, *Louis Pasteur* (London: Adam & Charles Black, 1957), pp 32–34, 45–47.
143. Adapted from *Encounter* (June 1993), p 5.
144. Adapted from James Edwin Orr, *The Second Evangelical Awakening in Britain* (London: Marshall, Morgan & Scott, 1949), pp 16–17.
146. Adapted from Knight, *Treasury*, p 41.
147. Adapted from Norman Grubb *C T Studd: Cricketer & Pioneer* (London: Lutterworth, 1933), p 91.
148. Adapted from 'To Illustrate . . .', *Leadership* 10 (#1, 1989), p 46.
150. Adapted from 'He's Back!' *The Bulletin* (12 September, 1989), pp 46–54.
152. Adapted from Dr David Burns, 'How to Conquer Anxiety', *Reader's Digest* (May 1991), pp 57–58.
153. Adapted from *Pulpit Resource* 4 (#1, 1987), p 10.
155. Adapted from, 'Laughter, The Best Medicine', *Reader's Digest* (August 1991), p 50.
156. Caroline Buchanan, 'I'll Never Have Sex Again', *Woman's Day* (22 August 1994), p 35.
157. Adapted from Tan, *7,700 Illustrations*, #7455.
158. Larry Crabb, *The Marriage Builder* (Grand Rapids: Zondervan, 1992), pp 103–5.
160. Deffner, *Seasonal Illustrations*, p 37.
161. Tan, *7,700 Illustrations*, #4908.
163. Adapted from Tom Walker, *From Here to Heaven* (London: Hodder and Stoughton, 1987), pp 131–132.
169. Adapted from Webb, *1001 Illustrations*, #14.
171. Adapted from *Parables, Etc* 14(#5, July 1994), p 5.
174. Adapted from MacDonald, *Ordering Your Private World*, pp 173–4.
175. Adapted from 'To Illustrate . . . ', *Leadership* 13 (#3, 1992), p 47.
176. Adapted from *Pulpit Resource* 4 (#1, 1987), p 19.
177. Jim Cymbala, 'Keeping Connected to Spiritual Power,' *Leadership* 14 (#4, 1993), pp 67–68.
178. Used with permission.
181. Adapted from Mitsuo Fuchida, *I Bombed Pearl Harbour* (Dee Why: PTL).
182. J Stevenson, *A New Eusebius* (London, SPCK, 1965), #24.

183. Adapted from Knight, *Treasury*, pp 77-8.
185. Woolmer, *Growing*, pp 93-5.
186. 'Changing of a Red Guard,' *The Sower*, No. 149, Special Edition (September 1994), p 8. A publication of the Bible Society in Australia Inc., Canberra.
187. Used with permission.
188. Adapted from *Encounter* (June 1993), p 5.
189. Adapted from Suzanne Muchnic, 'A Recovered "Fortune",' *Los Angeles Times* (29 April 1992), pp F1 and F6. (Copyright 1992, *Los Angeles Times*. Reprinted by permission).
190. Adapted from Ali Sougou, 'Challenging Settings Testimony II,' in J D Douglas (ed.), *Proclaim Christ Until He Comes* (Minneapolis: World Wide, 1990), p 136.
191. Adapted from F W Boreham, *Handful of Stars* (London: Epworth, 1922).
192. Adapted from *Pulpit Resource* 4(#2, 1987), p 25.
193. Adapted from Green, *Illustrations*, #1136.
194. Adapted from *Parables, Etc.* 14 (#2, April 1994), p 2.
195. Adapted from Webb, *1001 Illustrations*, #122.
196. Rowland Croucher, *Grow! Meditations and Prayers for New Christians* (Melbourne: JBCE, 1992), p 79.
198. Richard Wurmbrand, *Alone With God* (London: Hodder and Stoughton, 1988), pp 12-13.
200. Adapted from Murray Watts, *Rolling in the Aisles* (Eastbourne: Monarch, 1987), p 28.

Indexes

BIBLICAL PASSAGES

Genesis
1:1–2 14
3 71
4:10–16 143
4:23–24 143
9:5–6 143
15:1 .... 50, 53
18:1–15 73
18:1–8 69
18:19 .... 108, 110, 111,
112, 113, 117
19:1 69
22:18 .... 105, 106, 107
37:22–24 .... 28, 198
39:19–23 .... 28, 198
40:1–8 .... 28, 198
42:16–19 .... 28, 198
50:19–20 .... 28, 53
50:20 50

Exodus
3:1–6 73
6:6 ..... 8, 47, 48, 132, 146
13:21–22 .... 58, 59, 60
15:22–27 17
16:13 17
17:1–8 17
18 28
18:21 77
20:8–11 174

Exodus (cont'd)
20:13–14 154
20:13 61
20:14 .... 2, 3, 4, 29,
137, 200
22:1–3 74
22:20 108
22:21 69
31:12–17 174
32:8 108
32:14 29
33:14 .... 58, 59, 60
34:6 .... 42, 43, 44
34:15 108
34:27–28 .... 124, 125,
199

Leviticus
5:5 .... 29, 61
16:21 29
18:20 29
18:22 1
18:26 108
18:31 108
19:2 .... 18, 68
19:10 69
19:18 .... 5, 7, 9, 19, 143
20:10 ..... 2, 3, 4, 137, 200
20:13 1
23:3 174
26:40–42 .... 29, 61

Numbers
5:5–7 29
12:3 .... 70, 74
32:23 161
35:9–35 69
35:9–15 143
35:16–21 143
35:22–28 143

Deuteronomy
1:3 77
4:30 .... 58, 59, 60
5:16 .... 109, 110, 111,
112, 113, 117
5:17 61
5:18 .... 2, 3, 4, 29,
137, 200
6:4–9 .... 109, 110, 111,
112, 113, 117
6:20–25 .... 39, 40
10:19 69
14:1–2 18
18:2 70
18:10–13 108
22:22–24 29
23:3–4 69
24:1–5 .... 95, 96, 97,
136, 151, 153,
156
30:19–20 82

Deuteronomy (cont'd)

31:6	58, 59, 60
31:8	58, 59, 60
32:17	108
32:20	36
32:23	161
32:35	19
32:36	29

Joshua

10:13	143
20:1–9	69

Judges

2:18	29
6:17–23	69
8:5–17	69
12:3–6	143
13:15–21	69
16:21–25	28, 198
19:15	69

1 Samuel

3:1–4.1	73
15:22	105, 106, 107
18:1–5	90
19:1–8	90
25:2–38	69

2 Samuel

11–12	44
11	41, 42, 129
12	56, 57, 135
12:16–24	124, 125, 199
22:26	70

1 Kings

3:16–28	44, 143
8:22–53	94, 130
8:33–34	29
17	50, 53
18:30–40	128
19:11–12	58, 59, 60
22–23	11, 12
22:27	28, 198

2 Kings

4:8–10	69
9:7	143

1 Chronicles

21:16	29

2 Chronicles

6:1–42	130
7:14	29
16:10	28, 198
18:26	28, 198

Ezra

8:21	124, 125, 199

Nehemiah

1:6	29
3:25	198
8:10	30, 32
9:2	29
9:17	29, 42, 43, 44, 45
12:39	198
13:15–22	174

Job	31, 32, 38, 167, 171, 172
26:6	161
31:4	161
31:15	154
31:32	69
38:1–40.2	71
38:4–7	14
38:41	50, 53
40:6–41.34	71

Psalms

1	103, 162, 163, 164, 165, 176
4	131
4:8	145
5	131
5:5	173
6	131
6:5–7	56, 57, 135

Psalms (cont'd)

12	131
13	131
14:1	10, 11, 12
17:3	161
18:2	36, 37
18:35	70
19:1–4	13
22:9–10	154
23	6, 131, 167
23:4	57, 58, 59, 60, 135
25	131
25:1–4	58, 59, 60
25:9	58, 59, 60, 93
26:1	36, 37
27:1	53
27:14	19, 104, 169, 170
28	131
31	131
31:9–10	129
31:10	61
32	41, 42, 44, 46, 129, 181, 186
32:5	29, 61
32:8	58, 59, 60, 93
33:6	14
33:9	14
33:13–15	161
34	34, 35, 181, 186, 192
34:1	52, 81, 109, 115, 119, 129, 182, 196
34:4	56, 75, 166, 168
34:14	19
35	131
37:3–6	36, 37
37:3–5	51, 100
37:5	50, 53
37:23–24	50, 53
37:29	98, 99, 102, 197
38	129
40:12–17	131
44	131
46	56, 57, 75, 135, 166, 168

Psalms (cont'd)

48:14..........58, 59, 60, 93
51................. 29, 41, 42,
              46, 61, 94
52................................44
53:1..........................51
54..............................131
55:18........................145
55:22..........50, 53, 56, 57,
              75, 135, 152,
              154, 166, 168
56:4–5..................50, 53
59..............................131
61..............................131
62..............................131
64..............................131
66:12............. 58, 59, 60
69..............................131
69:10.......... 124, 125, 199
70..............................131
71:6 ....81, 109, 115, 119,
          129, 154, 182, 196
77..............................131
77:14–15 .... 8, 47, 48,
                    132, 146
89:46–52 131
90:2 14
91 ....31, 50, 53, 131, 192
94..............................143
100 ....179, 180, 181, 186
102:25 14
103:2–3 94
103:12........42, 43, 44, 45
106:45 29
108 131
112:9......49, 55, 123, 187
113:5–6 ....70, 74
113:5–9 13
118 192
118:5–6 31
118:6......50, 53, 152, 154
119:28 ....56, 57, 135
119:153–160 131
119:169–176 131
120 131
121 ....181, 186

Psalms (cont'd)

124 131
126 131
130 131
135:14 29
138:7.....................59, 60
138:58 58
139 ....154, 161
140 131
142 131
143 131
144 131
145:10–13 51

Proverbs

1:19 ....98, 99, 102,
                       197
3:5–6............ 50, 53, 58,
             59, 60, 100
3:5 ....36, 37
3:34 70
6:32 ....2, 3, 4, 137, 200
10:12...................89, 91
11:2 173
12:25 88
15:11 161
15:13 88
15:25 173
15:27 ..... 98, 99, 102, 197
15:33 ....70, 74
16:18–19 173
17:22 88
18:2 70
18:12 74
20:9 61
20:22 19
21:26...... 98, 99, 102, 197
22:6 18
25:6–7 70
28:13 29
29:18 194
29:25.............98, 99, 102,
            197, 134, 136, 157

Ecclesiastes

11:5 154

Isaiah

6:1–13 ....15, 77
7:14 ....51, 73
9:6–7 101
9:6 19
11:1–3 101
25:8 ....56, 57, 135
26:3 145
29:13–18 18
29:13..........................68
38:17........42, 43, 44, 45
40:12–26 51
40:22..........................14
40:26..........................14
40:28..........................14
42:2 ....59, 60
42:5 14
42:7 .... 28, 198
43:2 58
43:25..........42, 43, 44, 45
45:18..........................14
49:1 154
49:5 154
49:15 ....50, 53
52:13–53.12................78
53 .... 104, 169, 170
53:3–4 ....56, 57, 135
55:10 123
55:10–11 .... 49, 55,
                         187
58:5–12 199
58:7 69
58:12 ....124, 125
58:13–14 174
61:1 .... 32, 42, 43, 44, 45
64:8 .... 133, 138, 139,
             141, 142, 148, 175

Jeremiah

1:4–19 15
1:5 154
3:8 ....2, 3, 4, 137, 200
5:7 ....2, 3, 4, 137, 200
7:22–23 ..... 105, 106, 107
10:1–16 51

Jeremiah (cont'd)

10:12–16	*14*
12:3	*161*
13:27	*2, 3, 4, 137, 200*
14:11–12	*124, 125, 199*
17:19–23	*174*
18:8	*29*
20:9	*105, 106, 107*
21:8	*82*
23:5–6	*101*
23:24	*161*
26:3	*29*
26:13	*29*
26:19	*29*
31:9	*18*
31:34	*42, 43, 44, 45, 94*
32:2	*28, 198*
32:8	*28, 198*
32:12	*28, 198*
33:1	*28, 198*
37:16	*28, 198*
37:20	*28, 198*
37:21	*28, 198*
38:6	*28, 198*
38:13	*28, 198*
38:28	*28, 198*
42:10	*29*

Daniel

2:1–49	*185*
3:16–18	*19*
3:25	*58, 59, 60*
3:28	*58, 59, 60*
5:22–31	*70*
9:1–27	*45*
9:9	*29, 42, 43, 44*
9:19	*94*
9:20	*29*

Hosea

2:1–5	*2, 3, 4, 137, 200*
11:1	*18*
13:14	*56, 57, 135*
14:2	*81, 109, 115, 129, 182, 196*

Joel

2:12–13	*18, 68*
2:13–14	*29*
2:28	*59, 60, 119, 178*

Amos

9:2–4	*161*

Jonah

1:3	*161*
4:2	*29*

Micah

5:2	*101*
7:19	*42, 43, 44, 45*

Zephaniah

1:7	*69*

Zechariah

7:1–14	*124, 125, 199*
8:19	*124, 125, 199*

Malachi

1:6	*133, 138, 139, 141, 142, 148, 175*
2:10	*133, 138, 139, 141, 142, 148, 175*
3:8–10	*50, 99, 187*

Matthew

1:18–2.23	*150*
1:18–25	*101*
1:23	*51, 73*
3:6	*29*
5:4	*31, 56, 57, 134, 135, 136*
5:7–8	*2, 3, 4, 137, 200*
5:9	*145*
5:12	*16, 38, 81, 115, 119, 129, 131, 171, 172, 182, 196*
5:13–16	*84, 87*
5:14–16	*116*
5:16	*171*

Matthew (cont'd)

5:18	*10, 11, 12*
5:21–26	*39, 40*
5:21–48	*188*
5:22	*98, 99, 102, 197*
5:22–24	*19*
5:27–28	*136*
5:27–29	*95, 96, 97, 151, 153, 156*
5:27–30	*117, 159*
5:31–32	*95, 96, 97, 136, 151, 153, 156*
5:36–42	*143*
5:37	*76*
5:43–48	*19*
6:1–14	*128*
6:14–15	*44*
6:16	*74*
6:19–21	*55, 81, 192*
6:19–34	*75*
6:24–34	*192*
6:24	*98, 99, 102, 197*
6:25	*114*
7:13–82	*82*
7:21–27	*17*
8:5–13	*62, 63, 64, 65, 100, 185*
9:27–31	*62, 63, 64, 65, 100, 185*
10:1–15	*15*
10:16–20	*181, 186*
10:28	*192*
10:38	*75*
11:29	*37, 70, 78*
13:14	*24*
13:43	*171*
13:44–46	*189*
15:19–20	*18, 68*
16:27	*21*
18:21–35	*29, 41, 46, 61*
19:3–12	*95, 96, 97, 151, 153, 156*
19:9	*2, 3, 4, 137, 200*
23:37	*13*
24:11	*82*
25:1–13	*17*

Matthew (cont'd)

25:14–30 ....21, 30, 198
28:16–20 15
28:18–20 101
28:19.............................190
28:20..............................52

Mark

1:1–3.............................101
1:1 ....140, 193
1:7 70
1:12–13 86
1:14–15 184
1:15 .... 29, 114
1:16–20 83
1:21–28 ....34, 35, 164
1:29–31 ....62, 63, 64, 65,
100, 185
1:40–44 ....62, 63, 64, 65,
100, 185
2:1–12.......29, 36, 37, 41,
42, 44, 45, 62,
63, 64, 65, 94,
100, 158, 161, 185
2:14 83
2:15–17 69
2:18–22 ..... 124, 125, 199
2:27 174
3:1–6.........62, 63, 64, 65,
100, 185
3:7–12...........................93
3:13–19 77
3:13–15 .... 15, 101
3:20–27 165
3:35 129
4:18–19 ....98, 99, 102,
197
5:1–20............54, 35, 164
5:21–43 .... 26, 37
5:24–34 ....62, 63, 64, 65,
100, 185
5:36 36
6:1–6............................189
6:6–13 .... 15, 93
6:7–13 .... 77, 101
7:1–23 188

Mark (cont'd)

7:21 ......2, 3, 4, 137, 200
7:22 173
7:24–30 ....34, 35, 164
7:31–37 ....62, 63, 64, 65,
100, 185
8:22–26 ....62, 63, 64, 65,
100, 185
8:34–36 83
8:36 197
9:14–29 ... 34, 35, 36, 37,
164
9:33–37 70
9:49–50 .... 84, 87
10:2–12 .... 95, 96, 97,
134, 136, 151, 153, 156
10:11..............2, 3, 4, 29,
137, 200
10:17–31 .... 49, 55, 98,
99, 102, 123,
187, 192, 197
10:19.....2, 3, 4, 137, 200
10:21.............................83
10:45..........8, 23, 47, 48,
78, 92, 104, 132,
146, 169, 170
10:46–52 ... 36, 37, 62,
63, 64, 65, 100, 185
10:50............................160
10:52..............................67
11:1–4 46
11:20–24 .... 36, 37
11:22–24 .....31, 100, 123
11:25.........29, 41, 46, 61,
94, 134, 136, 181, 186
12:31......................5, 7, 9
12:41–44 ......49, 55, 123,
187
13:21–23 82
13:22...................... 25, 85
14:25–43 119
14:36..............................13
15:10....................... 54, 81
15:21–37 23
15:21–29 31
16:1–8 ....140, 193

Luke

1:5–2.40 150
1:16 70
1:26–2.20 101
1:52 70
2:10 .... 19, 30, 32
2:14 19
3:7–14...........................29
4:1–13...........................86
4:7 118
4:14 118
4:18 ....32, 42, 43, 44,
45, 72, 92, 109
4:18–19 184
4:22–30 189
6:12–13 15
6:20–22 .... 30, 32
6:24 ...... 98, 99, 102, 197
6:27–30 145
6:27–36 19
6:27–38 41
7:1–10 ....31, 100, 123
7:36–50 69
8:9–14..........................70
8:22–25 .... 31, 192
9:1–6........ 15, 77, 93, 101
9:46–48 70
9:57–62 83
10:1–20 ... 15, 77, 93, 101
10:20.......... 19, 179, 180,
181, 183, 186, 190
10:25–37 .... 5, 7, 133,
138, 139, 141,
142, 148, 175
10:27........,,,19, 31, 95, 96,
97, 104, 134, 136,
151, 153, 156, 169, 170
10:29–37 .... 69, 78
10:38–42 69
11:1–5 128
11:1–4 ....44, 129, 133,
138, 139, 142, 148, 175
11:1–13 51
11:4 41

237

Luke (cont'd)

11:5–13 ....126, 127
11:13 129
11:43 70
12:1–12 192
12:4–7 .... 50, 53
12:5 75
12:16–21 ......98, 99, 102,
197
12:22–24 .... 50, 53
12:22–31 ....75, 114, 166,
168
12:22–34 ....152, 154
13:1–5 ....4, 5, 6
13:1–17 185
13:10–17 .... 62, 63, 64,
65, 100
13:24 82
14:1–6 .... 62, 63, 64,
65, 100
14:7–14 70
14:15–24 .... 66, 151
14:33 24
15:1–7 .... 92, 133, 138,
139, 141, 142,
148, 175, 192
15:8–10 .... 1, 92, 133,
138, 139, 141,
142, 148, 175, 192
15:11–32 .... 13, 89, 91,
114, 133, 138, 139,
141, 142, 148,
175, 192, 195
16:13..... 98, 99, 102, 197
16:19..... 98, 99, 102, 197
17:3 41
17:6 ....36, 37
18:1–8 ....126, 127
18:9–14 ......70, 173, 181,
186
19:1–10 ....49, 55, 123,
133, 187, 192
19:10 .... 138, 139, 141,
142, 148, 175
19:11–27 .... 30, 194
20:46 70

Luke (cont'd)

23:34 19
24:1–12 ....140, 193
24:21 ....8, 23, 47, 48,
132, 146
24:45–49 15

John

1:1–18 ....78, 80, 101
1:2–4 16
1:3–9 .... 84, 87
1:6–9 70
1:11–12 189
1:12 .... 13, 18
1:14 72
1:29 ....8, 23, 47, 48,
132, 146
1:43 83
2:23 177
2:24 161
3:10 186
3:16 ....13, 37, 89, 90,
91, 180
3:17 101
3:19–21 .... 84, 87
4:1–42 177
4:13–14 27
4:24 51
4:46–54 ....62, 63, 64, 65,
100, 185
4:48 .... 36, 37
4:53 177
5:1–9 ....36, 37
5:31–36 .... 84, 87
6:2 177
6:26 177
6:29 .... 105, 106, 107
8:1–11 ..... 2, 3, 4, 29, 42,
44, 137, 200
8:12 .... 84, 87
8:31–36 ......8, 29, 47, 48,
132, 183, 190
8:34–36 .... 61, 94
9:1–34 ......62, 63, 64, 65,
100, 185
9:5 .... 84, 87

John (cont'd)

10:1–6 83
10:1–18 .... 133, 138, 139,
141, 142, 148, 175
10:7 82
10:9 66
10:11–18 .... 90, 91
10:25 10
10:27 ....58, 59, 60, 83
10:28–30 147
10:35 .... 11, 12
10:38 .... 36, 37
10:42 177
11 ....56, 57, 135
11:9–10 .... 84, 87
11:19 20
11:25–26 .... 62, 63, 64,
65, 66, 192
11:45 177
11:50 .... 104, 169, 170
12:3 70
12:9 177
12:35–36 .... 84, 87
12:37 177
12:46 .... 84, 87
13:1 .... 90, 91
13:34 9
13:37 .... 90, 91
14:1–6 .... 66, 185
14:1–4 19
14:6 .... 16, 72, 82, 181,
186
14:15–24 .... 95, 96, 97,
105, 106, 107, 153, 156
14:16 190
14:26 125
15:11 .... 19, 179, 180,
181, 183, 186, 190
15:12–17 146
15:12 9
15:13 .... 90, 91
15:17 9
15:18–19 52
15:19 13
16:12–13 125
16:13 .... 58, 59, 60

John (cont'd)

16:27 13
16:32–33 52
16:33 19
17:4 52
17:13 ....30, 32
17:23 13
20:1–31 ....140, 193
20:17 .... 133, 138, 139,
141, 142, 148, 175
20:28 80
20:30–31 ....36, 37
22:22 83

Acts

1:8 .... 15, 93, 101, 118
2:1–42 ...... 179, 180, 181,
183, 184, 186, 190
2:1–4 178
2:17 ....59, 60, 119
2:22 ....62, 63, 64, 65
2:38 ....29, 61
2:43 45
2:46 ....30, 32
3:12–26 184
3:19–20 178
4:7 118
4:8–12 184
4:14 118
4:30 ....36, 122, 128
4:30–31 144
4:31 178
4:32–37 187
4:33 118
4:36 110
5:12 ....62, 63, 64, 65
5:17 118
5:29–32 184
5:29 .... 95, 96, 97, 105,
106, 107, 151, 153, 156
5:41 ....38, 171, 172
6:7 .... 105, 106, 107
6:8–8.3 190
6:8 118
7:60 19
8:1–40 125

Acts (cont'd)

9:1–22 147
9:1–19 ...... 179, 180, 181,
183, 186, 190
9:4–5 ....38, 171, 172
9:17 178
10:9–16 ....59, 60
10:34–48 ....179, 180,
181, 183, 184,
186, 190
10:38 118
11:22–26 .... 20, 26, 81,
196
13:1–3 ....125, 184
13:4–12 177
13:16–41 184
13:22–23 101
13:47 ....84, 87
13:52 178
14:7–8 183
14:8–18 .... 62, 63, 64,
65, 177
14:9 ....36, 37
14:15–17 184
14:22 ....38, 171, 172
14:23 28
15:41 .... 20, 26, 81, 196
16:7 125
16:16–18 ....34, 35, 177
16:23–40 ....28, 198
17:22–33 27
17:22–31 184
17:23–30 51
17:24 14
17:30 29
18:10 52
19:11–20 ....34, 35, 109
19:10 29
19:20 177
20:7–12 177
21:27–22.29 .... 28, 198
22:3 21
26:18 72
26:20 29
26:23 87
26:43 84

Acts (cont'd)

27:22 ....30, 32
27:25 ....30, 32
28:7–10 177
28:30 .... 28, 198

Romans

1:1 32
1:3–4 ....140, 193
1:3 101
1:8–12 ...... 121, 122, 123,
124, 125, 126, 127, 144
1:16–3.20 .. 130, 191, 199
1:16 188
1:18–32 ....4, 5, 6, 85
1:18–20 ....51, 71
1:20 14
1:24–27 1
1:26–27 154
1:30 173
2:13 17
2:19 ....84, 87
3:19–31 ....33, 149
3:20 188
3:21–28 130
3:21–25 ..... 104, 169, 170
3:23 29
3:25 ....42, 44
4:14 188
4:18 16
4:21 177
5 94
5:1–5 .... 16, 19, 56,
57, 135
5:1–2 149
5:2–5 131
5:2 ....16, 66, 130,
191, 199
5:3–5 ....81, 115, 119,
129, 182, 196
5:3 ....38, 171, 172
5:7–8 ....90, 91
5:10 175
5:19 ....106, 107
5:12–21 72
5:18–19 .....62, 63, 64, 65

239

Romans (cont'd)

5:19 105
6:1–14 ...... 104, 162, 163,
           164, 165, 176
6:1–6 18
6:6 67
6:11 .... 18, 68
6:12–14 86
6:14–15 188
6:17 .... 105, 106, 107
6:19 .... 18, 68
6:23 .... 29, 94
7:14–23 .... 103, 117, 159,
      162, 163, 164, 165, 176
8:3 101
8:6 145
8:8–25 16
8:14–17 18
8:15 .... 13, 129
8:17–18 172
8:17 .... 133, 138, 139,
           141, 142, 148, 175
8:18 66
8:21 32
8:26 ..... 51, 126, 127, 128
8:26–28 57
8:28 .... 28, 50, 53
8:29 66
8:31–39 .... 6, 103, 109,
           138, 139, 148, 162,
           163, 164, 165, 176
8:38 28
9:31–10.3 .... 105, 106,
                              107
10:9 .... 130, 191, 199
10:15 145
10:16 .... 105, 106, 107
10:17 62
11:28 175
12 .... 54, 81
12:1–8 173
12:1–2 .... 105, 106, 107
12:2 14
12:3–8 174
12:5 74
12:6 .... 22, 29

Romans (cont'd)

12:9–21 19
12:10 .... 39, 40, 89,
                      91, 158
12:11 .... 21, 30, 198
12:12–31 173
12:12 ...... 16, 38, 75, 121,
       122, 123, 124, 125,
       126, 127, 144, 171, 172
12:13–14 69
12:14 .... 41, 46
12:16–18 .... 39, 40
12:17–19 143
12:18 145
12:20–21 5
12:20 145
13:4 143
13:9–10 9
13:9 .... 4, 5, 6, 7, 29
13:13 .... 21, 30, 198
13:14 67
14:7–8 .... 21, 81, 115,
           129, 182, 190, 196
14:17 145
14:19 .... 20, 26, 27,
                    81, 145, 196
15:1 20
15:13 .... 16, 145
15:19 177

1 Corinthians

1:3–7 6
1:10–17 145
1:18 118
1:30 ....8, 23, 47, 48,
                    132, 146
2:1–5 177
2:16 70
4:1–2 21
4:2 .... 30, 198
4:5 .... 84, 87
4:16 .... 74, 79, 80, 83,
           103, 162, 163,
           164, 165, 176
5:5 .... 150, 195

1 Corinthians (cont'd)

5:7 ....8, 23, 47, 48,
                    132, 146
6:9–18 1
6:13 154
6:19–20 .... 8, 47, 48,
                    132, 146
6:20 .... 74, 92
7:1–16 .... 136, 155
7:1–11 ..... 151, 153, 156
7:8–9 159
7:11 .... 95, 96, 97
7:15 .... 19, 145
7:16 134
7:22–23 .... 8, 47, 48,
                    132, 146
7:22 32
7:23 92
7:35 .... 82, 85
9:19 32
9:22–23 32
9:23–27 118
9:24–27 .... 103, 162, 163,
           164, 165, 176
10 ....152, 154
10:13 70
10:23 .... 20, 26, 81, 196
11:1 ....74, 79, 80, 83
11:29–32 46
12:1–13 152
12:8 .... 22, 36
12:9 .... 36, 62, 63, 64, 65
12:10 .... 22, 29
12:26–27 .... 38, 172
12:27 74
12:28 .... 22, 36, 62,
                      63, 64, 65
12:30 ... 36, 62, 63, 64, 65
13 .... 9, 19, 41, 89, 91,
       92, 95, 96, 97, 104,
       134, 145, 146, 151, 152,
       153, 154, 156, 169, 170
13:2 .... 22, 36
13:4–7 13
13:8 .... 22, 36
13:12 66

1 Corinthians (cont'd)

13:13 16
14:6 .... 22, 36
14:12 .... 21, 198
14:14–16 .... 121, 122, 123, 124, 125, 126, 127, 144
14:30 .... 22, 36
15 .... 66, 140, 193
15:12–35 195
15:19 16
15:22 .... 105, 106, 107
15:24 28
15:54–56 .... 56, 57, 135
16:13 .... 103, 162, 163, 164, 165, 176

2 Corinthians

1:3–11 31
1:3–7 .... 20, 38, 42, 56, 57, 134, 135, 136, 167, 171, 172
1:8–11 147
1:10 16
1:14 195
3:17 32
4:1–18 .... 147, 153
4:4–6 .... 84, 88
4:7–18 30
4:7–12 167
4:7 189
4:13 .... 191, 199
4:16 14
4:17 16
5:7 .... 67, 81
5:15 ... 115, 129, 182, 196
5:17 .... 14, 180, 188
6:4–10 30
6:5 .... 28, 198
6:16 18
7:1 .... 18, 68
7:6 167
8 .... 49, 50, 55, 101, 123, 187
9 .... 49, 50, 55, 101, 123, 187

2 Corinthians (cont'd)

9:8 116
10:1–6 ...... 103, 162, 163, 164, 165, 176
10:1 78
11:13–15 82
11:16–23 .... 153, 171
11:23 .... 28, 198
11:23–28 30
11:30 19
12:1–13 .... 81, 86, 154, 196
12:9–10 177
12:9 19
13:4 .... 140, 193
13:11 145
13:14 190

Galatians

1:4 72
2:16 ..... 33, 130, 149, 188
2:20 ... 13, 18, 68, 72, 81, 105, 106, 107, 115, 129, 182, 183, 190, 196
3:1–14 188
3:2 .... 62, 63, 64, 65
3:5 .... 62, 63, 64, 65
3:13 ... 8, 23, 47, 48, 104, 132, 146, 169, 170
3:18 188
3:24 32
3:26 .... 133, 138, 139, 141, 142, 148, 175
3:27 67
4:4–7 18
4:4–5 .... 8, 47, 48, 101, 132, 146
4:4 92
4:6 .... 13, 129, 190
4:18 .... 21, 30, 198
4:32 29
5:1 .... 8, 32, 47, 48, 132, 146
5:5–6 16
5:6 .... 191, 199

Galatians (cont'd)

5:9 29
5:13 21
5:16–26 .... 18, 54, 81, 103, 162, 163, 164, 165, 176
5:16–22 173
5:16–21 86
5:16–17 159
5:16–24 1
5:18 188
5:19–22 145
5:22 .... 9, 30, 32, 74
6:2 .... 5, 7, 19, 20, 41, 172
6:9 .... 21, 25, 30, 41, 81, 82, 85, 115, 116, 129, 182, 196, 198
6:10 69
6:15 14

Ephesians

1:5 18
1:7 .... 8, 23, 47, 48, 132, 146
1:8 16
1:9 19
1:11–12 66
1:15–19 .... 121, 122, 123, 124, 125, 126, 127
1:19–20 ...... 118, 140, 193
1:20–21 28
2:1–12 71
2:1–10 .... 14, 33, 67, 116, 130, 191, 199
2:3 159
2:8–9 .... 57, 149
2:8 94
2:10 ..... 18, 28, 47, 68, 74
2:11–21 92
2:12 16
2:18 66
3:8–10 28
3:12 66
3:14–18 .... 121, 122, 123, 124, 125, 126, 127

241

Ephesians (cont'd)

3:16–17 .... 103, 162, 163, 164, 165, 176
4:1 18
4:2 .... 9, 70
4:4 16
4:4–16 173
4:11 22
4:11–12 28
4:15 80
4:17–5.2 ... 103, 162, 163, 164, 165, 176
4:18 71
4:22–24 67
4:22 .... 86, 159
4:25–32 160
4:28 .... 21, 30, 98, 99, 102, 197, 198
4:29 .... 20, 26, 81, 196
4:32–5.2 .... 105, 106, 107
4:32 94
5:2 .... 8, 13, 44, 47, 48, 132, 146
5:3–14 160
5:3–5 .... 18, 68
5:3 .... 1, 154
5:8 .... 84, 87
5:13 .... 84, 87
5:18 178
5:20 ..... 52, 81, 109, 115, 119, 129, 182, 196
5:21–6.3 180
5:21–33 ..... 134, 136, 157
5:25 13
6:1 .... 110, 111, 112, 112, 117
6:1–4 .... 39, 40, 66, 109, 158
6:2 20
6:4 .... 109, 110, 111, 112, 113, 117
6:5 21
6:5–8 .... 166, 168
6:5–9 .... 30, 198
6:10–20 .... 103, 162, 163, 164, 165, 176

Ephesians (cont'd)

6:13–18 .... 121, 122, 123, 124, 125, 126, 127
6:18 .... 51, 114
6:20 .... 28, 198

Philippians

1:7 .... 28, 198
1:13 .... 28, 198
1:14 .... 28, 198
1:16 .... 28, 198
1:17 .... 28, 198
1:21 .... 81, 115, 129, 182, 196
1:29 .... 38, 171, 172, 191, 199
2:1 110
2:1–11 .... 70, 78
2:3–11 .... 181, 186
2:5 .... 74, 79, 80, 83
2:5–8 .... 105, 106, 107
2:5–11 80
2:11 153
3:7–9 24
3:9 188
3:10 ..... 38, 118, 171, 172
3:17 .... 74, 79, 80, 83
3:18 175
4:6 ...... 75, 114, 121, 122, 123, 124, 125, 126, 127, 152, 154
4:6–7 19
4:8 .... 117, 134, 136
4:11 147
4:12 .... 81, 115, 119, 129, 182, 196
4:13 19

Colossians

1:5 16
1:9–14 ...... 121, 122, 123, 124, 125, 126, 127, 144
1:10 .... 18, 21, 30, 116, 198
1:12 66
1:13 72

Colossians (cont'd)

1:15–20 .... 78, 80
1:21–22 175
1:24 167
1:27 16
2:9–10 28
2:13 29
2:13–14 94
2:15 .... 28, 72
2:19 80
3:1–17 ...... 103, 162, 163, 164, 165, 176
3:4 16
3:5 159
3:5–11 160
3:8–14 67
3:8 86
3:12 .... 9, 70
3:12–17 .... 18, 145
3:18–4.1 .... 157, 180
3:18–21 .... 39, 40, 158
3:20–21 ...... 66, 109, 110, 111, 112, 113, 117
3:23 .... 166, 168
3:23–24 .... 21, 30, 198
3:24 171
4:2 .... 121, 122, 123, 124, 125, 126, 127, 144
4:3 .... 28, 198
4:8 20
4:10 69
4:18 .... 28, 198

1 Thessalonians

1:2 .... 121, 122, 123, 124, 125, 126, 127, 144
1:2–3 16
1:5 .... 27, 62, 63, 64, 65, 177
1:6 .... 38, 74, 79, 80, 83, 171, 172
1:8 .... 106, 107
1:9 177
2:12 110
2:14 .... 74, 79, 80, 83
3:2 20

1 Thessalonians (cont'd)

4:1 18
4:1–8 68
4:3 .... 1, 154
4:6 143
4:9 .... 89, 91
4:11 .... 21, 30, 198
4:13 16
4:13–5:11 .... 150, 195
4:13–18 .... 56, 57, 135
4:18 20
5:3 16
5:5 .... 84, 87
5:11 .... 26, 81, 196
5:12 .... 20, 144
5:13 .... 19, 46, 145
5:14 .... 20, 110
5:16–18 .... 179, 180, 181,
186
5:17 .... 122, 126, 127
5:20 22

2 Thessalonians

1:8 105
2:1–12 150
2:2 195
2:16–17 .... 13, 20, 21
3:6 .... 79, 83, 137
3:7–9 74
3:9 .... 79, 83
3:10 .... 21, 198
3:16 145

1 Timothy

1:8–11 1
1:15 .... 24, 101
1:18 .... 103, 162, 163,
164, 265, 276
2:5–6 92
2:6 .... 47, 104, 169, 170
2:15 .... 18, 68
3:2 69
3:3 .... 98, 99, 102, 197
3:6 80
3:8 .... 98, 99, 102, 197
3:9 80

1 Timothy (cont'd)

4:1–5 155
4:11–13 21
4:12 .... 30, 198
5:10 69
6:6–8 147
6:10 .... 98, 99, 102,
192, 197
6:17–19 .... 48, 55, 98, 99,
102, 123, 187, 197

2 Timothy

1:7–8 118
1:7 .... 75, 192
1:9 149
1:16 .... 28, 198
2:9 .... 28, 198
2:21 .... 18, 21, 68, 116,
198
2:22 .... 19, 145, 159
3:5 137
3:12 .... 38, 171, 172
3:16–17 .... 10, 11, 12, 68,
119
3:16 .... 78, 181, 186
3:17 74

Titus

1:8 69
2:11–13 159
2:13 18
2:14 .... 8, 21, 23, 30,
47, 48, 68, 105,
106, 107, 116,
132, 146, 198
3:1–11 .... 33, 68
3:1 .... 18, 116
3:5 14

Philemon

10 .... 28, 198
13 .... 28, 198

Hebrews

1 29
1:1–14 .... 80, 101

Hebrews (cont'd)

2:4 36
2:9–18 101
2:18 .... 38, 171, 172
3:6 .... 16, 66
4:13 161
4:15 .... 171, 172
4:18 38
5:8 23
5:8–9 .... 105, 106, 107
6:10–12 16
9:15 ... 8, 47, 48, 132, 146
9:28 .... 104, 150, 169,
170, 195
10:4–14 101
10:6 51
10:30 19
10:34 .... 81, 115, 119,
129, 182, 196
10:36 .... 16, 19
11:8 .... 105, 106, 107
11:17 .... 105, 106, 107
12:1–3 .... 74, 79, 80, 83
12:1 160
12:3 .... 38, 171, 172
12:5 .... 38, 171, 172
12:9 .... 133, 138, 139,
141, 142, 148, 175
12:10 18
12:11 .... 38, 171, 172
12:14 .... 18, 68, 145
13:1 .... 9, 91
13:2 69
13:5 ..... 50, 55, 123, 147,
152, 154, 187
13:5–6 .... 75, 181, 186,
192
13:12 23
13:13 .... 38, 171, 172
13:14 16
13:15 .... 52, 81, 109, 115,
119, 129, 182, 196

James

1:2 .... 19, 31
1:2–4 .... 32, 56, 57, 81,

James (cont'd)

      86, 115, 119, 129,
      131, 135, 167, 171,
      172, 182, 196
1:2–14 .... *38*
1:5 .... *181, 186*
1:13–15 .... *86*
1:21 .... *86*
1:22 .... *17*
1:25 .... *30, 32*
2:2–4 .... *70*
2:8 .... *5, 20*
2:11 .... *29*
4:10 .... *70*
5:12 .... *76*
5:14–15 ..... *62, 63, 64, 65*
5:16 .... *29, 43, 44, 45, 61*

1 Peter

1:3–9 .... *16, 147*
1:6 .... *31, 131*
1:6–7 .... *38, 119, 171, 172*
1:7 .... *81, 115, 129,*
      182, 196
1:13 .... *16, 62, 63, 64, 65*
1:15–16 .... *18, 68, 105,*
      106, 107
1:18–19 .... *8, 23, 47,*
      48, 78, 132, 146
1:21 .... *16, 89*
1:22 .... *9, 91, 105,*
      106, 107
2:1 .... *67, 86*
2:5 .... *81, 109, 115, 119,*
      129, 182, 196
2:8 .... *105, 106, 107*
2:9 .... *84, 87*
2:11 .... *159*
2:12 .... *18, 68, 74*
2:15 .... *18, 68*
2:16 .... *32*
2:21 .... *23, 38, 74, 79,*
      80, 83, 171, 172
2:24 ..... *44, 104, 169, 170*
3:1 .... *105, 106, 107*
3:9 .... *19*
3:11 .... *19, 145*
3:14 .... *30, 32*
3:18 .... *23*
4:1 .... *23*
4:1–2 .... *38, 171, 172*
4:2 .... *18, 105, 106, 107*
4:3 .... *159*
4:8 .... *89, 91*
4:9 .... *69*
4:10 .... *21, 198*
4:12–16 .... *38, 171, 172*
4:13–14 .... *30, 32*
4:13 .... *52*
4:17 .... *105, 106, 107*
5:5–6 .... *70, 75*
5:7 .... *50, 53, 152, 154*
5:6–7 .... *56, 57, 135*
5:9 .... *38, 171, 172*
5:10 .... *31*
5:14–15 .... *100, 185*

2 Peter

1:3 .... *24*
1:3–21 .... *16*
1:19 .... *84, 87*
1:20–21 .... *10, 11, 12*
2:1 .... *25, 82, 85*
2:9 .... *16*
2:14 .... *2, 3, 4, 137, 200*
3:1–18 .... *150*
3:10 .... *195*

1 John

1:1–5 .... *78*
1:4 .... *30, 32*
1:5 .... *84, 87*
1:8–9 ... *29, 42, 43, 44, 45*

1 John (cont'd)

2:2 .... *8, 47, 48, 83,*
      132, 146
2:6 .... *74, 79, 80*
2:7–11 .... *9*
2:12 .... *29, 94*
2:15–16 .... *159*
2:15–17 .... *173*
2:22 .... *101*
2:27 .... *125*
2:28 .... *16*
3:2 .... *16, 66*
3:11–24 .... *9*
3:13 .... *52*
3:16 .... *90, 91*
3:17 .... *74, 78*
3:22 .... *105, 107*
4:1 .... *25, 82, 85*
4:2–3 .... *101*
4:7–11 .... *74, 83*
4:7–19 .... *13*
4:7–21 .... *9*
4:9–10 .... *90, 91, 93*
4.18 .... *88*
5:6–12 .... *79, 80*
5:7 .... *190*

2 John

7 .... *101*

3 John

11 .... *18, 68*

Revelation

1:10 .... *174*
6:10 .... *143*
16:14 .... *195*
19:2 .... *143*
21:4–5 .... *67*
21:23 .... *84, 87*
22:14 .... *30, 32*
22:25 .... *84, 87*

NAMES, PLACES AND THEMES

Abergavenny (ship)	161
Abortion	54
Abuse	1, 39, 45, 158
Achievement	21, 99, 197
Acceptance	5, 6, 9, 40, 41, 42, 43, 135, 149, 175, 177
Access	149
Achievement	21, 98, 99, 197
Actors	156
Adam and Christ	72
Addenbrookes Hospital	67
Adelaide	141
Adultery	2, 3, 4, 29, 41, 137, 200
Advent	19, 78, 92, 93, 101, 115, 146, 148, 150
Africa	26, 131, 162
AIDS	4, 5, 6
Airport, John F. Kennedy	25
Alberta	130
Alcohol	11, 177
Alienation	71
Alvarez, Mr.	100
Ambition	74
Angels	125
Anger	16, 21, 167
Annacondia, Carlos	164
Antioch	182
Anxiety	75, 114, 152, 154, 166, 168
Apprenticing	70, 83
Arabs	47
Argentina	27, 28
Arizona	118
Assurance	15
Atheism	38, 51
Athletes	15, 82
Atomic weapons	23
Atonement	44, 47, 48, 92, 104, 132, 148, 170
Australia	27
Austria	149
Authority	112
Avenger	143
Babies	13
Bad language	51
Baptist church	30
Barfield, Velma	61
Barnabas	26, 110
Basketball	4
Beauty	14
Belonging	9
Berg, Elizabeth	13
Berlin	195
Bernstein, Leonard	173
Bible	10, 19, 37, 68, 78, 97, 119, 185, 186
importance of	11
influence of	12
inspiration	10
life changing	11, 12
memorising	10, 78
reading	10, 28, 68

study	10
value of	6, 12, 78
Bikini (atol)	23
Bingham, Derick	123
Birmingham Repertory Theatre	73
Birth	13
Bishops	128, 182
Bitterness	16, 46
Blackfoot Indians	130
Blackwater fever	121
Blessing	27
BMW	10
Body of Christ	74, 173
Bolivar, Simon	48
Bolivia	48
Booth, Leon	11
Boredom	166
Born again	186
Bosnia	72, 138
British Museum	140
Broken(ness)	14, 42
Brooklyn, New York	114
Brotherhood	69
Brunei, Sultan of	197
Brussels	193
Buenos Aires	28
Bundy, Ted	117
Burden	20
Burns, David	152
Buxton, Paul	137
Call	15, 77, 105, 153
Canada	103
Canadian Pacific Railway	130
Cancer	16, 172, 196
Cannons	86
Cape of Good Hope	131
Capital punishment	61, 117
Care	7
Care for others	192
Carey, George	49
Career	77
Cars	10
Carter, President Jimmy	21
Cathedrals	103
Catherine the Great	188
Catholicism	103, 115
Cattle	100, 163
Celibacy	156
Cell groups	28
Central Park, Long Island	93
Chalmers, missionary	126
Change	17, 73, 180, 188
Character	86, 176
Cherokee Indians	171
Chicago	69, 91
Children	39, 40, 47, 95, 110, 111, 112
Children of God	18
Chile	59
China	30, 45, 186
Chlorophorm	24
Christ	
Body of	74, 173
imitation of	74, 79
Christian living	68
Christmas	19, 78, 92, 93, 101, 115, 146, 148
Christmas Carols	19
Chosen	15
Christie, Linford	70
Christies	189
Christmas	13
Church buildings	49
Church growth	28, 59, 105, 125, 144
Church planting	184
Clergy	6, 42, 94, 108, 114, 200
Coincidences	53
Coke, Bishop Thomas	107
Coleridge, Samuel Taylor	116
College	33
Comfort	20, 56, 57, 135
Commitment	21, 25, 96, 97, 107, 151
Communication	22, 97, 186, 198
Communism	41, 51
Communists	38, 106, 175, 186
Compassion	5, 6, 96
Confession	29, 43, 44, 61, 114, 161
Confidence – in God	16
Conflict	135, 136, 151
Congo	52

Consistency 76
Contentment 95, 147
Control 113
Conversion 11, 12, 29, 39, 100, 105,
    144, 147, 156, 177, 179, 180,
    181, 183, 184, 186, 190
Cook, Captain James 26
Cornish, David 178
Cornwall 65
Counsellors 11
Courage 17, 23, 82, 169, 170, 174
Court (law) 31
Courting 135, 154
Covent Garden 32
Cowboys 22, 100
Creation 14, 181
Creator 17, 181
Creativity 14, 116
Crete 84
Cricket 147, 179
Criticism 40, 91
Cross 8, 23, 31, 44, 47, 48,
    104, 132, 169, 170, 196
Crowfoot 130
Crucifixion 31
Crusades 105, 184
Cultural Revolution, The
    Chinese 30, 186
Cymbala, Jim 114

Damaged emotions 158
Dance 79
Darwin Award 118
Dating 135, 154
Death 2, 6, 7, 16, 56, 81,
    140, 145, 171, 193
Deception 85
Decisions 119
Defeat 193
Delcavo, Mike 82
Deliverance 34, 35
Demonic 34, 35, 97, 108
Demons 28, 34, 35
Denial 16
Depression 134, 178
Despair 135, 178

Dexter, Ted 179
Diary 152
Direction 118
Discipleship 15, 17, 25, 79, 83
Discipline 18, 39, 66, 113
Discouragement 110
Distractions 25, 82
Division 145
Divorce 97, 134, 137, 145,
    153, 156, 180
Domestic violence 151, 158
Dosso Dossi 189
Dostoevsky, Fedor 78
Doubt 100
Dreams 59, 185
Drug dealers 28
Drugs 11, 28, 61, 177
Duke of Windsor 18
'Dunamis' 118

East Germany 41
Easter 23, 92, 148, 169, 170, 193
Eastern Airlines 25
Edinburgh 23
Education 41
Edward VIII 18
Ego 173
Elders 28
Egypt 140
Election 15
Emotions – damaged 158
Encouragement 20, 26, 70, 110,
    169, 170, 196
Endeavour (ship) 26
Enemies 162, 163, 164, 165, 176
    love of 19, 103, 145, 175
Energy 118
Entertaining 69
Envy 54, 81, 173
Eschatology 32, 66, 150
Ethics 2, 3, 21, 35, 137, 200
Evangelism 5, 6, 15, 27, 92, 93,
    101, 123, 148, 171, 179,
    180, 183, 184, 190, 191
    power 29
    presence 30

247

Evil 28, 31, 32, 103,
    162, 163, 164, 165
Evil spirits 34
Examinations 33
Example 38, 83
Exodus, the 72
Exorcism 34, 35, 164

Expiation 8, 23, 47, 48, 132
Extortion 28

Failure 21, 105, 110, 116
Faith 36, 37, 60, 62, 65,
    83, 100, 105, 130
Faithfulness 38, 121, 156
Fall 71
Fallen creation 16
False
    leaders 25
    messiahs 85
    prophets 82
Fame 4, 70, 179
Family(ies) 9, 11, 39, 40, 45, 75, 92,
    93, 110, 135, 136, 151, 180
Farmers 124, 181
Fasting 124, 125, 127, 199
Fathers 40, 93, 110, 111,
    112, 113, 114, 158
Fatherhood 129
Fear 17, 19, 21, 53, 152, 160, 175
Fellowship of suffering 52
Ferre, Nels 80
Fifield, Paul 67
Fighting 145
Floods 60
Florida Everglades 25
Flying 25, 29, 83, 85, 118,
    148, 176, 181, 183, 197
Following 17, 21, 83
    Jesus 80, 82
Ford, Leighton 105
Forgiveness 12, 24, 28, 29, 40, 41,
    42, 43, 44, 45, 94, 159
Fornication 154, 156
Fossils 145
Frager, Chris 180

Franco-Prussian War 142, 195
Franz-Josef I 149
Frazer, James 165
Freeland, Kate 67
Freedom 8, 32, 45, 48, 67, 108
French Revolution 48
Frost, Leon 141
Fruit of the Spirit 30, 54, 74, 81,
    145, 159, 173
Funerals 6, 20, 149, 171
Future 194

Gaol 40
Geese 17
Gaboury, Adele 7
Gangsters 28
General Motors 75
Generosity 49, 50, 55, 98, 99, 197
Gifts 19, 33, 146
    of knowledge 22, 29, 36
    of Prophecy 22
    of Revelation 22
Gifts of the Spirits 22
Giving 49, 50, 55, 123, 187
Goals 106
God
    his call 15
    his care 37, 50, 53, 131, 187
    his creativity 14, 181
    discovering 51
    his existence 51, 180
    Father 129, 133, 138, 139, 142
    his favour 130
    his grace 57
    knowing 10
    listening to 58, 59, 60
    his love 5, 13, 42, 57, 72, 92,
    138, 139, 148, 180, 192
    meeting 5
    his nature 51
    omniscient 161
    as parent 13
    his power 34, 35
    his presence 52, 56, 57, 122,
    172, 180, 196

his provision 49, 50, 53, 54, 123, 187
    searching for 51
    his sovereignty
    his understanding 57
    voice of 73
    with us 51
Gold Coast 11
Good 103, 162, 163, 164, 165
Good news 140, 193
Good Samaritan 5, 6
Good Shepherd 133, 138, 139, 141, 142
Good words 46, 47, 74, 116
Gospel – its value 189
Gossip 86
Grace 94, 130, 149, 178, 199
    alone 191
Graham, Billy 8
Gratitude 146
Greatness 70
Greed 54, 55, 81, 98, 99, 197
Grief 20, 45, 56, 57, 80, 104, 172
Guidance 25, 28, 36, 37, 57, 59, 60, 93, 125
Guilt 29, 61, 94, 159, 161, 167, 168
Gulag 196

Habits 160
Habsburgs 149
Haiti 161
Hanoi 19
Hansberry, Lorraine 91
Happiness 95
Harper's (magazine) 150
Hatred 84, 147
Healing 34, 35, 36, 62, 63, 64, 65, 100, 129
    inner 1, 14, 39, 42, 45, 46, 94, 97, 158, 178
Hearsch, Robert 75
Heart transplant 104
Heaven 16, 66, 149
Heinz, John 92
Hell 66
Help 67

Hendley, Terry and Noleen 137
Hermits 128
Hero worship 4
Heroes 4
Hiding 161
HIV 4, 177
Holiness 18, 68
Hollywood 153
Holocaust 31
Holy Family 103
Holy Spirit 118, 125
    directing 125, 126
    filling 56, 178
Homosexuality 1, 5, 6, 108
Honeker, Erich and Uwe 41
Honesty 44, 198
Hoover, Willis 59
Hope 16, 66, 195
Hospital 11, 35, 104, 146, 153
Hospitality 69
Hugo, Victor 86
Humility 24, 70, 74, 149, 153, 173
Humour 2, 22, 33, 43, 60, 67, 76, 85, 95, 96, 100, 102, 106, 109, 111, 112, 118, 119, 134, 143, 150, 155, 157, 188, 198, 200
Hungary 153
Hurts 14
Husbands 95, 96

I am the light 84
Iby Saud 143
Ice Cream 134
Idols 4
Ignatius 182
Illness 62, 64, 167, 168
Imitation of Christ 74, 79, 83
Immorality 1, 3
Incarnation 71, 72, 73, 74, 101
India 169
Indian, American 22, 194
Inge, William 135
Inheritance 2
Injustice 75
Inner healing 1, 14, 39, 42, 45, 46, 94, 97, 158, 178

Integrity 41, 76, 77
Intercession 28, 121, 122, 144
Intimacy 45
Iran 14

JATO rocket 118
Jealousy 145, 173
Jesus
    his character 42, 70, 78, 106
    his death 23, 169, 170
    following 80, 82
    Good Shepherd 133
    the head 80
    imitating 79, 83
    the light
    most important 80
    his name 34, 35
    his work 8, 23, 44, 48, 72,
                     90, 104, 132, 175
John the Baptist 70
Johnson, Earvin 'Magic' 4
Journal 13, 50
Journalism 119
Joy 19, 30, 32, 38, 45,
                 64, 147, 179, 181
Judgement 81
Justice 113, 143

Kennedy, John F. 73, 101
KGB 141
Kidnapping 47
Kidney disease 63
Kierkegaard, Søren 17, 76
Kindness 5, 6, 74, 96
King Edward VIII 18
Kingdom of God 189
Kingston 161
Knowledge, Gift of 22, 29, 36
Korea 94

Lamberene Hospital 153
Language 10
Lanphier, Jeremiah 144
La Plata 28
Law 188, 199
    works of 33

Laying on of hands 63, 64
Laziness 116
Leadership ... 17, 21, 25, 26, 28, 42, 70,
    72, 77, 82, 83, 86, 130, 153, 194
    false 25
Legends 194
Lidford Brook 191
Life 11, 84, 103, 106, 109,
               162, 163, 164, 165
    after death 5, 66
    meaning of 12
    purpose 15, 153, 183
    storms 86
    troubles 175
    style 98, 99, 108, 197
Light 84, 171
Listening to God 58, 59, 60
Livingstone, David 68
Logic 33
London 85
Lord's Prayer 44, 46, 129, 133,
                   138, 139, 142
Los Almos 23
Love 4, 6, 9, 39, 40, 43, 91,
            92, 95, 96, 97, 104,
          134, 169, 170, 195, 199
    of enemies 145
    God's 5, 16
    for God 16
    of neighbour 20, 69
    of others 146, 181
    practical 93
Loyalty 86
Lust 159

McDonough, Ted 12
McCain, John 19
Mafia 28
Magic 108
Malaysia 64
Man 136
Marathon Monks 199
Marijuana 11
Marriage 4, 9, 16, 43, 45, 95,
          96, 134, 136, 145, 151,
         153, 155, 156, 172, 185

difficulties 61, 94, 97, 153, 158
    renewed 97
Marrian, Stephanie........................ 156
Martin, Steve 111
Martyrdom 52, 169, 170, 182
Martyrs 41, 115
Marxism 38
Masturbation 159
Materialism 47, 49, 55, 77, 81, 91,
                98, 99, 102, 147, 153,
                187, 192, 197, 198
Mayor.. 27
Media 117
Medicine 23, 34, 35
Memorization 78
Men 45, 134, 136, 156, 157
Mentoring.................................. 70, 83
Mercy 143
Messiahs
    false... 85
Methodist Church 59, 107, 141
Miami.......................................25, 148
Michigan 104
Mid-life crisis........................... 172, 178
Minnesota...................................... 124
Miracles 35, 36, 53, 62, 63, 64, 65,
            100, 123, 124, 125, 128, 150
Mirrors 14
Mission........................15, 77, 101, 164
Missionaries 35, 37, 52, 105, 107,
            121, 122, 125, 126, 147
Mission field 35
Mississippi 69
Mitsuo Fuchida 181
Modelling 38
Models 156
Money 47, 49, 55, 58, 70, 98, 99,
            102, 153, 177, 187, 197
Monks 128, 199
Moon landing 101
Moravians 122
Morillon, General Philippe.............. 72
Morse code 198
Moses 70
Mothers 13, 20, 38, 111, 112
Murder 28, 31, 61, 73, 117, 137

Muretus 192
Music 173
Muslims................... 105, 125, 185, 190

Nancy (ship) 161
Napoleon I, Emperor 193
National Basketball Association 15
National Geographic magazine 145
NATO 138, 139
Navy, The 19, 21, 161, 181
Nazis 84
Negativity 86, 91, 103
Neglect 7
Nehemiah 45
Neighbours 7, 20
New England 189
New Hebrides 37
New life.................... 12, 67, 103, 104,
                162, 163, 164, 165
New Life Ministry at Street
    Level 11
New nature 67
New South Wales 12
New York 25, 146, 150, 189
New York Philharmonic
    Orchestra 173
New Zealand 26
Nightingale 32
Noah 60
North Carolina 171
Norway.. 80
Nottingham Crown Court............. 137
Nuns 134
Nuremberg War Crimes
    Tribunal 31

Obedience 58, 59, 60, 105,
                106, 107, 120
Occult 108
Odessa 51
Offerings 49, 55, 187
O'Grady, Scott 138
Oklahoma 135, 171
Old age.. 107
Old life 67, 86, 103, 160, 162,
                163, 164, 165, 176

Old nature 67, 86
Olmos Prison 28
Olympic Games 70
Opportunities 14
Optimism 109
Orchestras 173
Oxford 157

Paige, Handley 176
Pain 16
Paintings 189
Palace 14
Palau, Luis 184
Papaderos, Dr Alexander 84
Parables 17, 76
   Friend at Midnight 126, 127
   Good Samaritan 5, 6, 69, 133,
      138, 139, 141, 142, 175
   Great Banquet 66
   Lost Coin 133, 138, 139,
      141, 142, 192
   Lost Sheep 133, 138, 139, 141,
      142, 175, 192
   Pearl of Great Price 24, 189
   Pharisee and the Tax Collector
      70, 173
   Prodigal Son 40, 71, 91, 114,
      133, 138, 139, 141,
      142, 192, 195
   Rich man and Lazarus 197
   Talents 21, 194, 198
   Ten Virgins 17
   Treasure 189
   Two Houses 17
   Unforgiving Sevant 41, 46
   Unjust Judge 126, 17
Parachutes 139
Pardon 94
Parenthood (film) 111
Parenting 3, 13, 18, 38, 39, 40, 61,
   66, 80, 91, 109, 110, 111, 112,
   113, 114, 117, 151, 158, 180
Paris 18
Parliament 174
Past 160
   hurts 14

Pasteur, Louis 142
Paul – opponents 145
Parton, John 37
Peace 16, 19, 56, 79, 145, 167, 185
Pearl Harbour 181
Pennsylvania 133
Pentecost 178
People, value of 138, 139, 192
Persecution 28, 38, 52, 78, 115,
   120, 125, 135, 147,
   169, 170, 171, 182, 196
Perseverance 21, 105, 106, 115, 116,
   126, 127, 131, 147, 176
Personal devotions 10
Persistence 21, 105, 106, 115, 116,
   126, 127, 131, 147, 176
Peru 184
Pessimism 109
Pets 111
Phips, Sir William 103
Plymouth Harbour 26
Police 7, 8
Politicians 174
Poor, the 50
Pornography 117, 159
Positive 109
Poverty 102, 192
Power 118
Power
   encounter 27, 34, 35, 45, 62,
      63, 64, 65, 100, 164
   evangelism 29
   in weakness 196
Practicalities 119
Praise 51, 109, 115, 120
Prayer 16, 27, 28, 36, 37, 58, 62,
   63, 64, 65, 94, 100, 114,
   121, 122, 131, 144, 164, 165
   answers 15, 51, 121, 122,
      123, 124, 128, 144
   constant 51, 57
   and fasting 124, 125
   first 51
   Lord's 44, 46, 129,
      133, 138, 142
   persistence 126, 127

unanswered 62, 129
vigils 28, 122, 124, 127, 144
simple 128
Preaching 17, 27, 200
Preachers 17
Predestination 15
Pregnancy 13
Prejudice 135
Preminger, Marion 153
Pressure 75
Pride 71, 173
Principalities and powers 28
Priorities 25, 119
Prison 19, 28, 38, 40, 120, 198
Prisoners 28
Promises 26
not accepted 130
Prophecy 22
Prophets
false 82
Prosperity 98, 99, 197
Prostitution 28, 94
Protection 72, 130
Psychiatrists 11, 39
Psychiatry 34, 35
Psychologists 112
Punishment 113
Purity 117
Purpose 17, 70, 77, 98,
99, 101, 106, 153

Quebec 103
Queen, British 197
Queensland 11
Questions of life 23

Rabbis 79
Ransom 8, 23, 132
Rathman, Tom 160
Ready, Pamela 63
Reality 9
Recommitment 16
Reconciliation 8, 46, 84, 114, 132,
133, 141, 175, 186
Recreation 14, 42
Redeemed 8, 47, 48, 132

Refreshment 174, 178
Regis, John 70
Regulations 188
Reincarnation 199
Rejection 9, 40, 41, 52, 69, 134, 180
Relationships 9, 16, 134,
135, 136, 156
Religion 39
false 137
Renewal 97, 178, 183
Repentance 29, 61, 108, 114
Representative 23
Rescued 47, 48, 72, 92, 132,
138, 139, 148, 175
Resistencia 27
Rest 174
Resurrection 118, 140, 193
Retirement 70
Retribution 84
Reunion 141, 142
Revelation, gift of 22
Revenge 143
Revival 59, 144, 164
Reward 26
Riches 102
Rickover, Admiral Hyman 21
Rigoletto (opera) 170
Riots 28
Rivalry 145
Robertson 139
Roddan, Ron 70
Rome 182, 192
Rosevere, Dr Helen 52, 172
Rubbish tip 12
Russia 79, 188

Sabbath 174
Sacrifice 23, 41, 77, 104, 169, 170
Sacrifical giving 49, 55, 187
Safe sex 4
Saib, Tippo 169
Saints 68
Salt and light 84
Salvation 60, 72, 104, 133, 138, 139,
141, 142, 148, 149, 175, 191
rejected 130

253

Sanctification 18, 68
Satan 28, 39
Satanists 164
Saved 148, 149
Schweitzer, Albert 153
Scientists 23, 58
Second Coming 150, 195
Secretaries 39
Self esteem 151, 152
Self image 151, 152
Selfishness 137
Separation 80, 97, 172, 185
Serbia 72
Servant 78
Servant evangelism 7, 27, 74, 93
Service 70, 74, 153, 173
Sex 1, 4, 13, 45, 154, 15, 156
Sexism 157
Sexual abuse 1, 158
Sexual ethics 4
Sexual fantasies 35
Sexuality 2, 3, 137, 159, 200
Shame 41, 45
Sheik, Bilquis 185
Ships 26
Shock 16
Shopping 20, 134
Siberia 78
Sickness 62, 64, 96
Signs and wonders ... 62, 63, 64, 65, 100
Silvoso, Ed 27, 28, 45, 100
Simplicity 128
Simpson, Sir James 24
Sin 24, 29, 40, 61, 85, 137, 160
   disclosed 161
Singing 171
Singleness 159
Sjogren, Steve 93
Slavery 32, 57, 48, 174
Slotin, Louis 23
Small groups 28
Snakes 160
Snow White 95
Solomon
   wisdom of 44, 143
Solzhenitsyn, Alexander 196

Sons of God 18
Sonship 18
Sougou, Ali 190
South America 48. 164
South Australia 3
Sovereignty of God 53
Space race 101
Sparrow (ship) 161
Spirit, fruit of 30, 54, 74, 81,
                                  145, 159, 173
Spirits 34, 35
Spiritual battle 28, 103, 162, 163,
                                  164, 165, 176
Spiritual warfare 28, 103, 162,
                                  164, 165, 176
Sport 4, 70
Srebrenica 72
Standard Oil 77
Stanley, Sir Henry Morton 68
Stanley, Paul 175
Stealing 44, 113
Streenburgen, Mary 111
Storms 86
Steadman, Ray 53
Stephen 190
Stress 75, 110, 166, 167, 168
Strong Man 165
Studd, CT 147
Students 33, 106
Submarines 21
Submission 106
Substitution 23, 104, 145, 146, 169
Success 21, 70, 105, 110
Suffering 16, 19, 20, 23, 30, 31,
                              32, 34, 35, 38, 52,
                              75, 104, 106, 115, 120,
                              129, 131, 146, 147, 167,
                              169, 170, 171, 172, 182,
                              196, 198
Suicide 11, 56, 135, 183
Sultan of Brunei 197
Sunday 174
Support 70
Surrender 175
Svarinskas, Father 115
Sympathy 20

Szmaglewska, S. 31
Szuber, Chester 104

Tahiti... 26
Taylor, Hudson 50
Teaching 70
Teachers... 44
Teenagers 112, 180
Tehema Wildlife Area................... 160
Tehran 14
Television 16
Templemann, Rebecca 129
Temptation 86, 176
Ten Commandments 200
Terelya, Iosyp................................. 115
Testimony 177, 190
    David Cornish...................... 178
    Ted Dexter............................ 179
    Chris Frager.......................... 180
    Mitsuo Fuchida 181
    Ignatius.................................. 182
    Sake Kobayashi 183
    Rosario 184
    Bilquis Sheik 185
    Ying Gao 186
    Scott O'Grady...................... 138
Thanksgiving 109, 131
Theatre... 73
Theft 44, 113, 200
Thirst 27
Tithing 49, 55, 187, 197
Toilets 102
Toronto Blessing 122
Tokyo 94
Toys 9
Tradition.. 188
Tragedy............ 25, 31, 83, 85, 104, 171
Trains 74, 102
Translation 37
Travelling 2
Treasure found 189
Trinity 190
Triumphal Entry 150
Triumphant 19
Trust........ 36, 37, 67, 83, 100, 130, 195
Tsar 188

Tunstall, John 34
Twelve Steps to Recovery................ 11

U–235 23
Unemployment 75
United Nations 72
Unity 79
University 33
Urgency 191
Urquhart, Colin and Caroline.......... 65

Value of people 192
Vasco de Garma 131
Velveteen Rabbit, The 9
Vengeance 143
Verdi, Giuseppe............................. 170
Victory 72, 193
Vienna 153
Vietnam War............................ 19, 175
Violence... 117
Vision 17, 59, 106, 194
Visions.......................... 36, 42, 120

Waiting 195
Walker, Tom 163
Walking on water 128
Wall Street (film)............................. 55
Walley, Major 103
War 19, 31, 84, 142, 149
Warsaw 141
Water... 27
Waterloo, Battle of........................ 193
Weakness 152, 196
Wealth 49, 55, 81, 99, 102,
                         187, 192, 197
Wellington, Duke of...................... 193
West Side Story 173
White, Dr. John 1, 64
Widow 2
Wilberforce, William 174
Wilkinson 140
Williams, Debbie........................... 139
Wills 2
Wimber, John.................................. 29
Wisdom 44, 143
Witchcraft 39

255

Witnessing 38, 171, 183, 190
Wives 95, 96
Women 136, 157
Wooton, Ebenezer 191
Work 2, 30, 75, 149, 166, 168, 191, 198, 199
Works of the flesh 54, 81, 199
Works of the law 33, 199
World War One 149
World War Two 84, 181, 183
Worship 4, 69, 80
Worry 50, 53, 75, 152, 154, 168
Wurmbrandt, Richard 38, 120, 198

Writing 116
Wyatt, Jr, Walter 148

X-Rated 200

Ying Gao 186
Young, Nicholas 26
Youth 56
Youth ministry 1, 154
Youth worker 1

Zeal 21
Zinzendorf, Count 122